Animals, Immortal Beings

Scriptural Evidence of the Immortality of Animals

Edited and with Commentary by

Mary Buddemeyer-Porter

Additional Commentary
with Scripture by

- Martin Luther
- John Calvin
- John Wesley
- George MacDonald
- Pope John Paul II
- and others

EDEN PUBLICATIONS, LLC
P.O. Box 7ᵒᵒ
Manchester,
www.creati
www.creaturesil

Second Printing

Copyright 2005 by Mary Buddemeyer-Porter

ISBN # 0-9746277-2-0

Cover illustration by Roman Buddemeyer and Crystal Wood

Eden Publications, LLC
P.O. Box 789
Manchester, MO 63011
www.creatures.com
www.creaturesinheaven.com

Contents

Acknowledgments

I want to thank the following people for their
research and encouragement.

Thanks to Margaret Miller, for sending me wonderful resource
books and material and encouraging me in every way.

Thanks to Robert S. Clark, for his efforts in finding original writings by various Christians.

Thanks to Bill LaSalle, for his support and commentary on *Animals, Immortal Beings.*

Thanks to Roman Buddemeyer, illustrator, for the cover design.

Thanks to Ronald Porter, for all his help in finding resources and
checking out the authenticity of various theologians' writings.

Thanks to Diane Pomerance, Ph.D., for her support and advice.

Thanks to Crystal Wood of Tattersall Publishing for editing and
formatting *Animals, Immortal Beings.*

Thanks to Eric and Debbie Freesmeier for their prayers.

Thanks to Don and Pam Close, for their support and for the
appearance of their cat, Coach, on the cover of *Animals, Immortal
Beings.* (The beagle represents our beloved Duffy.)

Thanks to Roger Fritz, who not only made my first book possible,
but made *Animals, Immortal Beings* happen.

Thanks to my family and those friends who have so prayed for this
ministry and have encouraged me in every way.

— MBP

Acknowledgments

The author is grateful to the authors and editors of many previously published works for material quoted herein under the doctrine of "fair use." Such references are credited in the text and in the bibliography at the end of this book.

In addition, the author has requested and received written permission to quote at length from the following works:

Animals, Nature, and Albert Schweitzer
    edited by Ann Cottrell Free
Crossing the Threshold of Hope and *God, Father, and Creator*
    by Pope John Paul II
The Dead Sea Scrolls Uncovered
    by Robert Eisenman and Michael Wise
Heaven's Countryside by Robert S. Clark
The Spirit of the Animal by the Rev. Jeff Harker
The Theology of the Book of Revelation
    by Dr. Richard Bauckham
Merciful God, Merciless Man by the Rev. James Carroll
The Cross of Jesus by Leon Morris
Virginia Christian Israelite Prayer by Robert A. Everett

Foreword

Several much-needed works have been written about the eternal life of animals. This is an important book because it will take you into the past to hear what highly respected theologians have had to say about animal immortality. Their conclusions will bring added reassurance to anyone who has turned to the church for comfort and walked away heartbroken after hearing the biblically unsound dogma that "animals have no eternal soul" and are without hope of eternal life.

Why do they think that way? Tom Harpur, writing in the *Toronto Star*, states that "some, of course, are scandalized on either intellectual or religious ground with such hopes."

The ground they stand upon has no foundation and gives out under their feet. The weight of truth enunciated by biblically learned men of the past such as Martin Luther, John Calvin, John Wesley, Albert Schweitzer, and Pope John Paul II of our generation puts an end to this modern error and low view of God's everlasting love for His animal creation.

Mary Buddemeyer-Porter has synthesized their teaching into a very readable book. Let's hope this book finds its way into the hands of every pastor, priest, and church member. If you have lost a pet, take heart.

— *Brian Dougan*

Brian Dougan is currently teaching
English in Daegu, South Korea.

Introduction

*A*nimals, Immortal Beings features commentary and scriptural references by some of the most noted of past and present Christian theologians and men of God. The book speaks of their lives, both personal and professional, and their stand concerning the salvation of man and restoration of all creation back to God.

Included in the book is a brief overview of some of the other religions and their laws concerning the treatment of animals.

In reference to commentary throughout the book, please note that when you read the initials *MBP*, it is the author's commentary you are reading within the commentary of the theologians featured.

As a Protestant having accepted Jesus Christ as my personal savior almost forty years ago, it is my prayer that all Christians and all those seeking God will learn through scripture included in *Animals, Immortal Beings* the messages of truth God so wants the world to know. That is the message of LOVE: love for God and His Son Jesus Christ, love for each other, and love for God's creation. The reward for that LOVE is eternal life with God and His creation in heaven.

Though the various Christian denominational founders and leaders agree that animals do have immortality, many disagree concerning the salvation of man. Within *Animals, Immortal Beings* you will find testimony that unites the basic understanding of the different faiths. All agree that only through the grace of God can man be saved, and only by redemption through Jesus Christ, and the forgiveness of our sins can man gain eternal life in heaven. Whatever the confusion and fear Protestants and Catholics may have of one another's Bible, one will find when reading them that God's truth still remains the same.

God has made it clear to me that my ministry is to reach all people and to use the tools God has provided to me to get the message of animal immorality and the salvation of mankind to the world. It is my sincere and humble prayer that within these pages you will learn truths, receive comfort and joy, and have a new, enriched personal relationship with our heavenly Father. He did so love the world that He gave His only begotten son to die for our sins and to restore creation back to Himself.

— *Mary Buddemeyer-Porter*

CHAPTER 1

The Assurance of the Gospel

A Prayer of St. Catherine of Siena:
The reason why God's servants love God's creatures so deeply is that they realize how deeply Christ loves them and love begets love in all eternity.

References:
- C.S. Lewis, ed., *George MacDonald, An Anthology of 365 Readings*
- George MacDonald, *The Hope of the Gospel*

George MacDonald was born in 1824, attended King's College at Aberdeen, and was called into the ministry in 1850. He was married and struggled his entire life to provide as best he could for his family. His family lived for the most part in poverty; MacDonald had diseased lungs and his ministry was to a large extent misunderstood. He therefore had to rely on lecturing, writing, and doing odd jobs to support his family, yet he lived in a state of today, not resting in dreams of the future. He rested instead in what he called "the holy Present."

George MacDonald was close to God from his earliest childhood and much respected as a devout Christian proclaiming the Gospel of Jesus Christ. He believed from his childhood that animals had immortality. He asks, "Are you the lowest kind of creature that could be permitted to live? Had God been of like heart with you [in other words, if God were like us], would He have given life and immorality to creatures so much less than himself as we? Are these (the lower creation) not worth making immortal? How, then, were they worth calling out of the depth of non-being?"

In *George MacDonald,* Reading #254, he speaks of the beasts and states: "The ways of God go down into microscopic depths as well as up to telescopic heights...So with mind; the ways of God go into the depths yet unrevealed to us: He knows His horses and dogs as we cannot know them, because we are not yet pure sons of God. When through our son-ship, as Paul teaches the redemption of these lower brothers and sisters shall have come, then we shall understand each other better. But now the Lord of Life has to look on at the willful torture of multitudes of His creatures. It must be that offenses come, but woe unto that man by whom they come! The Lord may seem not to heed, but He sees and knows."

In *The Hope of the Gospel,* George MacDonald wrote extensively on the eternal life of animals, focusing mainly on Romans 8: 18-23. "For we know that the whole creation groaneth and travaileth in pain together until now." (Romans 8:22 KJV) MacDonald interprets that to mean the apostle Paul regarded the whole visible creation as, in far differing degrees of consciousness, "a live outcome from the heart of the living one, who is all and in all; the word 'creature' or 'creation' must include everything in creation that has sentient life (those animals capable of suffering). Paul speaks of the whole creation as suffering in the process of its divine development, groaning and travailing as in the pangs of giving birth to a better self, a nobler world. It is not necessary to the idea that the creation should know what it is groaning after, or wherein the higher condition constituting its deliverance must consist. The human race does not know its own lack, or to have even a far-off notion of what alone can stop its groaning. In like manner the whole creation is groaning after an unforeseen yet essential birth, being freed to another state of being. In both the lower creation and the higher, this same groaning after a freer life seems the first enforced decree of a holy fate, and itself the first movement forward to the liberty of another birth.

"A god who would make the lower creatures only for prey with cruel masters torturing and killing them, a creator who endlessly creates creatures only to have them die for no self-good whatsoever, would not be the God we know of creation but a demon. But a creative demon is an absurdity.

"As for the child: Will the knowledge that their pet will soon die suffice for the heart of the child who laments over his dead bird or rabbit, and would gladly love that Father in heaven who keeps on making the creatures? Alas, as some would say concerning the creatures: they cannot help themselves; their misery is awaiting them! Would those Christians have me believe in a God who differentiates creatures from himself, only that they may be the prey of other creatures, or spend a few hours or years, helpless and lonely, speechless and without appeal in merciless hands, then pass away into nothingness? I will not; in the name of Jesus, I will not [believe such]. Had God not known something better, would He have said what he did about the Father of men and the sparrows? What many men call their beliefs are but the prejudices they happen to have picked up."

MacDonald goes on to say that the teachers of the nation have unwittingly wronged the animals deeply by their silence and the thoughtless popular presumption that animals have no hereafter, thus leaving them deprived of a great advantage to their position among men.

"For what good, for what divine purpose is the Maker of the sparrow present at its death, if He does not care what becomes of it? What is he there for, I repeat, if he has no concern that it goes well with His bird in its dying, that it be neither comfortless nor lost in the abyss? If His presence be no good to the sparrow, are you very sure what good it will be to you when your hour comes? I could not blame you for thinking all was over with the sparrow; but to believe in immortality for yourself, and not care to believe in it for the sparrow, would be simply hard-hearted and selfish.

"I know of no reason why I should not look for the animals to rise again, in the same sense in which I hope myself to rise again—

3

which is, to reappear, clothed with another and better form of life than before. If the Father will raise His children, why should not He also raise those whom he has taught His little ones to love? Love is the one bond of the universe, the heart of God, the life of His children: if animals can be loved, they are lovable; if they can love, they are yet more plainly lovable: if love is eternal, how then should its object perish? And if God gave the creatures to us, that a new phase of love might be born in us toward another kind of life from the same fountain, why should the new life be more perishing than the new love? I know no reasonable cause or difficulty in regard to the continued existence of the lower animals, except for the present nature of some of them. But what Christian will dare to say that God does not care about them? And He knows them as we cannot know them."

Concerning Romans 8:19, MacDonald said, "To come closer, if we may, to the idea that burned in his heart when he (Paul) wrote what we call the eighth chapter of his epistle to the Romans. Oh, how far ahead the apostle Paul seems in his hope for the creation. He knew Christ, and could therefore look into the will of the Father. For the earnest expectation of the creature waiteth for the manifestation of the sons of God."

MacDonald goes on to quote the heading of a poem from Henry Vaughan: "'For the things created, watching with head thrust out, await the revelation of the sons of God.' Why? Because God has subjected the creation to vanity, in the hope (assurance) that the creation itself shall be delivered from the bondage of corruption into the glorious liberty of the children of God. For this double deliverance—from corruption and the consequent subjection to vanity, the creation is eagerly watching. The bondage of corruption God encounters and counteracts by subjection to vanity. The suffering is for redemption, for deliverance. It is the life in the corrupting thing that makes the suffering possible; it is the live part, not the corrupted part, that suffers; it is the redeemable, not the doomed thing, that is subjected to vanity.

"So the hope of creation is that the creation shall share in the deliverance and liberty and glory of the children of God. Deliverance from corruption. liberty from bondage, must include escape from the very home and goal of corruption, namely death, and that in all its kinds and degrees. When you say then that for the children of God there is no more death, remember that the deliverance of the creature is from the bondage of corruption into glorious liberty as the creation is to share in the deliverance and liberty and glory of the children of God.

"The sons of God are not a new race of sons of God, but the old race glorified; why a new race of animals, and not the old ones glorified?

"What lovelier feature in the newness of the new earth, than the old animals glorified with us, in their home with us—our common home, the house of our Father—each kind an unfailing pleasure to the other! Ah, what horses! Ah, what dogs! Ah, what wild beasts, and what birds in the air! The entire redeemed creation goes to make up St. Paul's heaven.

"Would it not be more like the King eternal, immortal, invisible, to know no life but the immortal? To create nothing that could die? To slay nothing but evil? 'For he is not a God of the dead, but of the living; for all live unto him.'

"St. Paul seems to believe that perfection in their (the animals) kind awaits also the humbler inhabitants of our world. Its advent is to follow immediately on the manifestation of the sons of God. For our sakes and their own they have been made subject to vanity; for our sakes and their own they shall be restored and glorified, that is, raised higher with us.

"The word 'adoption' from St. Paul's writing means 'the redemption of the body.' The thing St. Paul means in the word he uses has simply nothing to do with adoption—nothing whatever. In the beginning of the fourth chapter of his epistle to the Galatians, he makes perfectly clear what he intends by it. His unusual word means the father's recognition when he comes of age, the child's relation to him, by giving him his fitting place of dignity in the house. And the deliverance of the body is the act of this recognition by the great Father, completing and crowning and declaring the freedom of the man, the perfecting of the last lingering remnant of his deliverance. St. Paul's word, I repeat, has nothing to do with adoption; it means manifestation of the grown-up sons of God."

MacDonald speaks of labor, death, and torture. "Labor is a law of the universe, and it's not an evil. Death is a law of this world at least, and is not an evil. Torture is the law of no world, but the hell of human invention. Labor and death are for the best good of those that labor and die; they are laws of life. Torture is doubtless over-ruled for the good of the tortured, but it will some day burn a very hell in the hearts of the torturer."

MacDonald speaks of the New Creation in Reading 126. "When the sons of God show as they are, taking, with the character, the appearance and the place, that belong to their son-ship (heaven); when the sons of God sit with the Son of God on the throne of their Father; then shall they (the creation/creatures) be in potency of fact the lords (man) of the lower creation, the bestowers of liberty and peace upon it: then shall the creation subjected to vanity for their sakes, find its freedom in their freedom, its gladness in their son-ship. The animals will glory to serve them, will joy to come to them for help. Let the heartless scoff, the unjust despise! The heart that cries *Abba, Father*, cries to the God of the sparrow and the oxen; nor can hope go too far in hoping what God will do for the creation that now groaneth and travaileth in pain because our higher birth is de-layed."

[In a 1957 edition of *Readers Digest*, "A Child Blessed," a story was told of the Apostle John, who had observed Christ while on earth comforting a little boy whose dog had just died. The story is told in *Will I See Fido in Heaven?* Jesus was observed telling a little boy whose dog lay dead at his feet that though the dog had departed its body it was not dead. Jesus used a seashell for his example to the little boy and said: How a small shell could house a living creature, which would depart its body, yet not die. Jesus told the weeping boy that animals see beyond this world in which man also dies. — MBP]

In Reading 314, "The Eternal Now," MacDonald says, "The bliss of the animals lies in this, that on their lower level, they shadow the bliss of those—few at any moment on the earth—who do not 'look before and after and pine for what is not' but live in the holy carelessness of the eternal now."

He continues, saying, "To those who expect a world to come, I say, then, Let us take heed how we present ourselves to the creation which is to occupy with us the world to come. To those whose hearts feel compassion for creation, I say, The Lord is mindful of his own, and will save both man and beast."

[A number of people have asked me if God takes the animals' spirit and soul, the immortal part of them, back to heaven, just as He does humans who are redeemed. They, as well as man, will get a new perfect body, which will never decay or die, just like the perfect bodies God created which Adam's and Eve's sin corrupted. The new heaven and the new earth are a renewal of the present one. God does not destroy one and make another one. — MBP]

CHAPTER 2

The Soul and Spirit of Man and Animal

References:
- Dr. Andrew Linzey, *Animal Theology*
- Reverend Jeff Harker, *The Spirit of the Animals*
- Robert Eisenman and Michael Wise, *The Dead Sea Scrolls Uncovered*
- Matthew Henry, *Commentary*
- Leon Morris, *The Cross of Jesus*

Concerning the soul and spirit of animals, the most credible of all the Greek and Hebrew scholars unequivocally agree that in every passage of Scripture where the Hebrew word *nephesh* or the Greek word *psyche* is used, it should be translated *soul*. When *nephesh chayah* is used it should be translated *living soul*. Most translations of the Bible for the past two hundred years translate "soul" as "being or living being."

Many people tend to see animals as some type of animated being that has no mind or ability to reason and does not feel any pain; nor can they love those of the human race or their own species. They cannot accept that both non-human beings and humans are all animals. Yet many accept that animals have a soul and spirit, which means they have a mind, the ability to feel pain, and have the ability to, and in fact do, make decisions and choices. They therefore see a connection with man and the lower animals, believing they are, in essence, akin to human beings. In science, man is classified as an animal, and when it comes to the workings of the body, many of the animal kingdom below man is strikingly related (however, that does not imply a form of evolution). Each species is created exactly the way God designed them and for the purpose God designed them to function. Man, unfortunately, has successfully altered much of creation to the detriment of all.

The thought by many people that all flesh has a body, soul, and spirit, as the Bible says, is unacceptable, and the thought of the word "animal" as denoting both man and beast is repulsive to them. Such arrogance is sad for mankind and tragic for the animals.

In *Animal Theology*, theologian and university professor Dr. Andrew Linzey states that animals are spirit-filled, living creatures. They have *theos*-rights, which means God-rights. They have the right to be what they are and to be treated with respect as God's creatures. Dr. Linzey says that when we control a creature for our own selfish purposes, ignoring its purpose in creation, we fall into sin.

Reverend Jeff Harker, theologian and minister of the First Baptist Church in Columbia, Indiana, did extensive research on the spirit and soul of the animal after reading *Will I See Fido in Heaven?* which proposes that animals do have a soul and spirit. *The Spirit of the Animals* is his wonderful research and commentary on the subject.

The Spirit of the Animals

Introduction

"I always thought I responded well to criticism," related Joni Eareckson Tada, "that is until my book *Heaven—Your Real Home* went to press." She went on, "I received more critical letters over one paragraph on page fifty-five than all totaled for anything I'd ever written. I penned it innocently enough: 'Animals in heaven? Yes. I think animals are some of God's best and most avant-garde ideas; Why would He throw out His greatest creative achievements? I'm not talking about my pet schnauzer, Scrappy, dying and going to heaven—Ecclesiastes 3:21 puts the brakes on that idea. I'm talking about new animals fit for a new order of things."

Joni's suggestion that earthly pets would not be in heaven produced an overflow of angry letters from Christian pet owners. As a result of the assault, she took a closer look at passages such as Ecclesiastes 3:21 to see if she really had a scriptural basis for her position on animal afterlife. After closer examination of Scripture, her view had definitely changed. "If God brings our pets back to life, it wouldn't surprise me. It would be totally in keeping with His generous character." She went on to say that she wasn't asserting that animals have souls or spirits. But the question that we should ask, as Bible students, is "What does the Scripture teach?" What will study of the Biblical message reveal? Does the Bible *teach* that animals do not have souls or spirits?

The truth of the matter is that, through the centuries, most Christians have accepted the theory that animals do have immaterial souls or spirits. It wasn't until the eighteenth century "Age of Enlightenment" and the thinking of men like Descartes and Hobbes that the existence of animal souls was even widely questioned in Western civilization. Throughout the history of the Christian church, the classic understanding of living things has included the doctrine that animals, as well as a humans, have an immaterial component to their essential being. [Gary R. Habermas & J.P. Moreland, *Beyond Death* (Crossway Books, 1998), p.107.] This general understanding declined during the period of the 1700s. This period of "enlightenment" brought agnosticism and skepticism to much of Christian culture, emphasizing scientific method and rationalism as a basis for proving all truth. During this period much general thinking on spiritual issues began to follow the principle of "omnicompetence of human reason" and argued that the basic ideas of Christianity, being rational, could be derived from reason itself. As a result of this tragic thinking there was a general rejection of biblical truth, and numerous commonly held beliefs fell by the wayside. [Alister E. McGrath, *Historical Theology* (Blackwell Publishers, 1998), p. 221.]

The most common Christian belief two hundred years later is that animals do not have souls or spirits. Although this view is widely accepted in Western Christian circles, a Bible student should question whether this view is sustained by Scripture. When Biblical passages are examined thoughtfully and taken literally, there seems to be compelling evidence that the animating life-element of an animal with nostrils is an immaterial spirit or soul. Upon further investigation of relevant passages, it is the opinion of this Bible student that the Scripture points even to the possibility of resurrection and restoration of much of the animal world. However, this short paper is limited to the issue of whether an animal possesses an immaterial nature.

Remember that the issue should never be what we might think or feel, but instead what God has revealed in His Word. Also remember throughout this study that "every word of God is purified (lit.)" by the all-knowing mind of God Himself (Prov. 30:6). This means, then, that the Scripture cannot be studied using a literal, grammatical, historical approach unless the Scripture is *translated* literally, with the exception, of course, of cultural idioms and other such grammatical constructions. Readability, thought flow, and other factors must take a back seat to the original text and original languages when such precision is required for understanding. The only approach which is fully credible is the approach taken by the apostle Paul, "What does the Scripture say?" This obviously requires an approach to the original Hebrew and Greek of the Bible in its historical and cultural contexts. A "King James Only" approach or an attitude of snubbing helpful translation tools when attempting to arrive at the original meaning of the Biblical text will not suffice in technical studies of this type. Our goal is to understand the original languages of God's Word.

Before we begin looking at the animal world at the time of Noah's flood, a brief introduction is necessary regarding the primary Biblical words used for *soul* and *spirit*.

Part I: Animal Souls or Spirits?

At the start, please understand that it is important to recognize that a person, a human being, does not actually *possess* a soul, but instead that he *exists as a soul* who inhabits a physical body. This is directly stated in Scripture: "The first man, Adam, became a living soul (*psyche*)." (1 Cor. 15:45, NASB) We observe from Scripture that a human being lives as a "soul" who inhabits a physical body, described figuratively in the Bible as a "tent." (2 Cor. 5:1-6) Therefore the "soul" is not something a person possesses *in addition to* life. Neither does the Bible teach the common misconception that the soul is an entity which is strictly associated with redemption, and therefore different from the "spirit."

Although this Bible student does not feel that "soul" and "spirit" are identical in all contexts, I do feel they are often used interchangeably when the distinction is not in view contextually. The original languages of the Bible use both "soul" and "spirit" to designate the very essence of life or the person himself. The Bible also teaches that this life element remains fully functional apart from the body after physical death (Lk. 16:19-31, Eccl. 12:7), while the body is said to "sleep" in the grave. When a Christian dies physically he leaves his physical body and becomes "absent from the body" while being "present with the Lord." (2 Cor. 5:8)

We see that in the resurrection of the just, for example, Jesus Christ will bring the immaterial soul, i.e. the Christian, with Him from heaven to join the individual to his resurrected body which has been "asleep" in the grave (1 Thess. 4:14-18). Therefore, instead of stating that man has a soul, it is much more Biblically correct to state that "man has a body"! Precisely, man should not be viewed as a material being who possesses an immaterial soul or spirit. Instead, man is viewed, Biblically, as a *spiritual being* who possesses a physical body. This is very important. In considering the animals, we are therefore obviously asking whether the very life-element of an animal is material or immaterial. In other words: Is an animal an immaterial being inhabiting a physical body paralleling the human situation? Or is an animal merely a self-contained set of biochemical processes?

The Hebrew vocabulary of the Old Testament did not contain a word that corresponds to the term "soul" in the sense of an immaterial life distinct from the physical body. In other words, "soul" in the Old Testament (Heb., *nephesh*) was not understood to exist apart from the body, whether referring to man or animal. However, the Old Testament did use a word (*ruach*) which, in reference to man, refers to an immaterial component. Nevertheless, it is clear that, with respect to man, there were two common Hebrew words sometimes used in the sense of "spirit" or "soul," and in certain contexts are universally translated this way.

In the Old Testament the primary word used for the English word "spirit" is *ruach*. Conversely, "spirit" is also by far the most common translation of the Hebrew word *ruach*. A good Hebrew lexicon such as Brown-Driver-Briggs will show a secondary translation to be "wind," while a still less common translation would be "breath," the context being the most critical factor. For example, in the King James Version *ruach* is translated "spirit" 232 times. It is translated "wind" ninety-three times, and "breath" only twenty-seven times. Note carefully, then, that in the great majority of Biblical cases the word *ruach* is used in some sense of *spirit*. Standard principles of translation would tell us, then, that *ruach* could possibly be used by the Lord in the sense of "spirit" in contexts where this makes good sense, unless there are other solid linguistic or contextual reasons for doing otherwise.

Sometimes the context is not clearly determinative, and so the translator must make a translation decision. For example, in Psalm 104:29, the NASB translates *ruach* "spirit," while the NIV translates the same word "breath." Here lies the real nature of the spirit/soul issue using English translations.

A corresponding problem occurs with the Old Testament Hebrew for "soul." There are two common English words that translate the Hebrew word *nephesh* (being, soul), another word which is also used for the essence of life in both men and animals (see Gen. 2:7 for example). *Nephesh* is sometimes translated "life" or "being" or "creature," while at other times it is translated "soul." If the context is not clearly decisive, the translator must resolve the issue using other criteria. This translation decision forms the nature of the problem in the spirit/soul issue. Yet, in the final analysis there seem to be several key Biblical passages that are conclusive in deciding whether animals possess immaterial life. Let us look at several of these key passages.

Genesis 7:21-22 (NASB): *"All flesh* that moved on the earth perished, birds and cattle and beasts and every swarming thing that swarms upon the earth, and all mankind; of all that was on the dry land, *all in whose nostrils was the breath of the spirit of life,* died. Thus He blotted out every living thing that was upon the face of the land, from man to animals to creeping things and to birds of the sky, and they were blotted out from the earth."

In this passage we see that "all flesh" includes birds, cattle, animals, and man. Abiding within each creature, including man, was "the breath of the spirit of life." (NASB, NKJV) The Hebrew reads *nishmat ruach hayyim. Nishmat* is from *neshamah,* a word used almost exclusively for literal breathing in the Old Testament. Note that this "breath" is associated with a "spirit of life." This is not apparent from the KJV & NIV translations, the two most common English translations used in Western culture. Both of these translations attempt to modify the full Hebrew expression by following the Greek Septuagint and the Latin Vulgate. Both of these omit "spirit of." Every student of the original languages of the Septuagint or Vulgate understands that neither of these translations is a "formal-equivalent" translation. A formal-equivalent translation would read, "in whose nostrils was the breath of the spirit of life." (NKJV, NASB) The prepositional phrase "in whose nostrils" (v. 22) refers to "all that was on the dry land." Therefore, this clearly refers to the animals in addition to man.

As you read this passage carefully, notice that it refers to "all flesh" that moved on earth (v. 21), describing these creatures as "all in whose nostrils was the breath of the *spirit* of life." (NASB, NKJV) "Breath" is *neshamah* and therefore speaks of the air-breathing function of these creatures, which resides in their "nostrils." The word translated "spirit" (*ruach*) is the word which is frequently used to speak of the very essence of life within a man, that is, his natural spirit. This passage by itself, therefore, *could* possibly speak of an immaterial spirit which belongs to these air-breathing animals. Note carefully that these creatures are characterized in the same manner as man with regard to "flesh" and "spirit." (v. 21) In other words, a "*spirit* of life" is associated with the flesh of animals as well as with the flesh of men. The implication is that the element of life in an animal may possibly be a living "spirit" rather than simply a set of biochemical processes. Speaking of animals as well as men, Young's Literal Translation translates the Hebrew this way: "...all in whose nostrils is breath *of a living spirit*—of all that is in the dry land—have died." (Gen. 7:22 YLT)

Again, notice that Genesis 7:22 is describing both man and animals. Also observe that *ruach*, the term used for *spirit* with respect to these animals, is distinct from the breath itself. As Vine's Expository Dictionary states, "In these verses the animals have a spirit." (*Vine's*, p. 241, Copyright 1985) This reliable Bible study tool goes on to state that *ruach* (spirit) also appears to be equivalent to the Hebrew term used for "soul" (*nephesh*) in passages such as Prov. 16:2. More will be said on this in a moment.

Because of the fact that "God is spirit" and man is the only creature described as being "in the image of God," some scholars have concluded that, since man is the only creature in the image of God, he is the only creature that can have a spirit. In effect, they are assigning equivalency to these two particulars without Biblical authorization. For example, Gleason Archer, normally a superb and very careful scholar, states: "It is usually understood that the spirit of man is the focal point of the divine image in man..." [*Encyclopedia of Bible Difficulties*, Zondervan, 1982.] However, this cannot be derived from the Bible, which does not actually teach or authorize this equivalency.

One of the finest Bible teachers I have personally heard teach the Word of God is Dr. John C. Whitcomb, former professor of Old Testament Theology at Grace Theological Seminary and co-author of *The Genesis Flood* with Dr. Henry Morris. It is the opinion of this writer that Dr. Whitcomb has also made this error. He has taught that animals have no eternal soul or spirit. Yet, this position seems to lack a solid Biblical basis. On the other hand, it is the opinion of this student that, when the Scriptures are translated literally and the evidence is allowed to speak, some very interesting things emerge and point more strongly toward the opposing view.

Although animals are not created "in the image of God," it appears that the Lord, who "forms the spirit of man within him," may possibly form spirits within air-breathing animals. Backing up to Genesis 6:17, we again see that a certain "spirit of life" resides in these animals. Again, the word used is *ruach.* In this verse it is sometimes translated "*breath* of life," but in light of Moses' initial use of the word *neshamah* for *breath* in Gen. 2:7 and its similar use of it again in 7:22, it would seem preferable in 6:17 to translate *ruach* "spirit," especially since both 6:17 and 7:22 refer to the same historical event described by the same writer, Moses. Also, as mentioned before it should be noted that *ruach* was used in the Scriptures in some sense of "spirit" *ten times more frequently* than in the sense of "breath." (See Brown-Driver-Briggs Hebrew lexicon.) This is very important.

After exhaustive study, it is the opinion of this student that Moses probably never used the word *ruach* in the sense of "breath" anywhere in His biblical writings, although it is clear that other Biblical writers did so, yet infrequently. The student who has a working knowledge of Biblical Hebrew is encouraged to examine this possibility carefully.

Young's Literal Translation makes the distinction clearly: "And behold, I Myself am bringing in the deluge of waters on the earth to destroy all flesh, *in which is a living spirit,* from under the heavens." (Gen. 6:17) This verse provides additional evidence that the life-element of an animal could very possibly be that of "a living spirit." Even when such technical distinctions between *ruach* and *neshamah* are not observed by the translator, breathing animals are nevertheless said, in this passage, to possess "the breath of life," showing us that they apparently possess a similar type of element to that which makes man a living being as stated in Genesis 2:7. It appears that in Genesis 6:17 in Young's literal translation may very well be correct in observing the distinction: "And behold, I Myself am bringing in the deluge of waters on the earth to destroy all flesh, *in which is a living spirit*, from under the heavens." (Gen. 6:17 YLT)

In addition to this Biblical data on "spirit," the Bible also suggests that an animal possesses, or more correctly, *exists as* a soul. (It will be shown that *spirit* and *soul* are often used with little or no differentiation and that both refer to some aspect of immaterial life.) Both man and animal are said to exist as a *nephesh*, the Old Testament term used for "soul" (Ps. 6:3, Ps. 19:7). *Nephesh* is the Hebrew equivalent of the New Testament *psuche*, the Greek term used for "soul" (Matt. 16:26, Matt. 10:28). Both the Hebrew noun *nephesh* and the Greek noun *psyche* refer to the very essence of life and are the normal Biblical words that translate "soul." The use of *nephesh* for animals is seen in Gen. 1:21 and 1:24 and should be compared with Gen. 2:7 which refers to man. It seems evident, once again, that these verses also indicate that an animal's basic life-element *could be* immaterial. We must make sure to examine other relevant passages, particularly passages that may be determinative. First, let us take a look at the similarities in these passages on *nephesh*, normally translated "being," "creature," or "soul."

Are Man and Animals Both Described as "Souls"?

(MAN): "...and the man became a *living creature* (*chay* = living, *nephesh* = being, creature, soul)" (2:7) Note: The NASB interprets this as "a living soul." (1 Cor. 15:45, NASB)

(ANIMALS): "...an abundance of *living creatures* (*chay* = living, *nephesh* = being, creature, soul) (Gen. 1:21)

(ANIMALS): "...bring forth the *living creature* (*chay* = living, *nephesh* = being, creature, or soul) according to its kind, cattle and creeping things and beasts of the earth." (v.24)

Notice carefully how these verses, contained in the foundational book of Genesis, suggest the *possibility* that these living creatures also possess "living souls." The evidence for an animal possessing immaterial life becomes even stronger when we observe that the Bible often attributes the same qualities and the same actions to both *soul* and *spirit*. Isaiah, for example, puts *nephesh* and *ruach* in synonymous parallel: "With my soul (*nephesh*) I have desired You in the night, yes, by my spirit (*ruach*) within me I will seek You early." (Isa. 26:9) Here, Isaiah equates the *soul* and the *spirit*. Further biblical comparison of the terms *spirit* and *soul* often yields no consistent difference between the terms. The Bible often uses the two terms interchangeably. For example, Job spoke of both "the anguish of my spirit" and "the bitterness of my soul" in the same verse (Job 7:11), while David wrote, "My soul is in anguish" (Ps. 6:3) and Asaph described his spirit as "embittered" (Ps. 73:21). Jesus said, "Now my heart (literally, "*soul*") is troubled" (John 12:27), yet John reported that "Jesus was troubled *in spirit*" (13:21). These and many other references show that the words *spirit* and *soul* are often used interchangeably. Although these two terms may, at times, refer to *different aspects* of the immaterial being, they nevertheless still seem to refer to the same immaterial nature. Therefore it should not be surprising that, since the Bible suggests that an animal is actually a living spirit (e.g. Gen. 7:22, NASB), it would also point to the possibility of its existence as a living soul (Gen. 1:20, 24, cp. 2:7).

Although some Christians will acknowledge the existence of the animal soul or spirit, they often attempt to say that the animal's spirit consists merely of a consciousness that results from the body's biochemical processes, and so they say that when the animal's bodily functions cease the soul or spirit also ceases. In other words, the soul or spirit is a concept or "metonymy," but not an actual entity. This seems to be based on preconceived bias rather than on what the Scripture actually says.

In his book, *Resurrection*, Hank Hanegraff indirectly cites Thomas Aquinas as having said that "animal souls function in clear dependence on the animal body." Although Hanegraff personally believes in the possibility of animal resurrection, he cautiously concludes that "because the soul of an animal is qualitatively different from the soul of a human, there is reasonable doubt that it can survive the death of its body." Here is my comment: While it is plausible for an animal soul to be, in some way, "qualitatively different," it does not follow that an animal soul is dependent on the body for its existence or "survival." Aquinas' comment appears to be pure speculation, as there is no Biblical evidence that an animal's soul or spirit could not function apart from the body. The following Scriptural evidence would seem to strongly suggest the opposite.

Ps. 104:29 is embedded in another context which suggests even more strongly that the life-element of an animal is an immaterial "spirit" (*ruach*) which comes from God (cf. Gen. 7:22, 6:17, Heb. text). This *ruach* of the animal is said to be "collected" or "gathered" (Heb. = *asaph*) by the Lord when the animal dies. The context of Psalm 104 is speaking of many types of creatures on earth and in the sea, wild and domesticated. Then it speaks of the physical death of these animals in verse 29. This verse appears to refer to both immaterial and material components of animals. The NASB translates, "You take away their spirit (*ruach*), they expire and return to their dust."

The word "take away" is *asaph*. The Brown-Driver-Briggs primary definition for *asaph* is "to gather" or "to collect." This is the lexical concept of *asaph* in all its Hebrew verb forms. In contrast, modern American English might say that the Lord "takes away" the animal's breath as if He were to cause it to "cease." But this concept is not present in the Hebrew text. The Hebrew concept is to "take away" by collecting or "gathering." Young's literal translation reflects this definition:

"You gather their spirit (*ruach*). They expire and return to their dust." (Ps. 104:29, YLT)

The New American Standard Bible, very highly respected among conservative Bible students and scholars, also observes some kind of animal "spirit" in this verse:

"You take away *their spirit*, they expire and return to their dust." (Ps. 104:29, NASB)

Comparison of various translations of Ps. 104:29 shows a tendency to translate *ruach* "breath" in order to avoid the implication that the life-element of an animal is an immaterial spirit which the Lord receives at the time of death. A typical translation will read: "You take away (*asaph*) their breath (*ruach*), they die and return to their dust," even though "spirit" far more frequently translates *ruach* in the Old Testament. In light of previous study in this paper, it seems far better to translate *ruach* "spirit," as in the New American Standard Bible or Young's Literal Translation. This is especially true when *asaph* is given its normal, literal meaning of *collect* or *gather*, since it would make much more sense for the Lord to collect an animal's spirit when it dies than for Him to collect the animal's breath! Although Psalm 104:29 does not reveal how the Lord might dispose of the animal spirit or what he may do with it, it states clearly that the Lord collects (*asaph*) the animal's spirit at the time of physical death.

Psalm 104:29 is the most important of all the passages which use *ruach* in connection with animals. The student who is familiar with Hebrew vocabulary should note that this verse does not say the Lord causes the *ruach* to stop or cease (e.g. *chadal*), but that it is "gathered" or "collected."

Once again it seems evident from this verse that a living animal is not merely a walking biochemical machine. Biblically, we see that "spirit" is associated with "all flesh" that has nostrils (e.g. Gen. 7:22, lit.), and the Lord receives the animal's spirit at the time of death as the body returns to the ground (Ps. 104:29, NASB). If an animal does exist as an immaterial spirit, and this does appear to be the case, then this gathering is exactly what we would expect from an omniscient God who controls all things. As Job 12:10 tells us, "In [the Lord's] hand is the life of every living thing, and the breath of all mankind."

Commenting on Psalm 104:29, Dr. Charles C. Ryrie, author of the *Ryrie Study Bible*, with typical precision in his Biblical analysis, comments: "The spirit of every living thing depends upon God's Spirit." (*NASB Ryrie Study Bible*, Expanded Edition, p. 926.) Those of us who have had the privilege of studying under Dr. Ryrie or studying his works know that his choice of the term "spirit" rather than "life" was deliberate. Here, Dr. Ryrie alludes to the Biblical implication that man may not be the only fleshly creature existing as a soul or spirit.

The "spirit of the animal" is also spoken of directly in Eccl. 3:21. The context is explaining how injustice demonstrates that people are similar to animals: "Concerning the condition of the sons of men, God tests them, that they themselves may see that they are like the animals." (Eccl. 3:18-21 NIV)

Man's fate is like that of the animals; the same fate awaits them both: As one dies, so dies the other. All have the same breath [NIV Study Bible: or "spirit" (*ruach*)]; man has no advantage over the animal. Everything is meaningless. All go to the same place; all come from dust, and to dust all return. Who knows if the spirit of man rises upward and if the spirit of the animal goes down into the earth?"

Notice this passage affirms that humans and animals both come from the same dust of the earth. Although man is the only creature "in the image of God," note in particular that animals are animated by the same life breath (v.19, cf. Job 34:14-15; Ps. 104:29) and that their bodies go to the same place, that is, return to the dust (Eccl. 3:20). The word translated "breath" in v.19 is *ruach*, which could also be translated "spirit," as footnoted in the NIV study Bible. Solomon argues that man has no advantage over an animal, because both are transitory from an earthly point of view. This context is speaking of ways in which animals and humans are alike. Verse 21 speaks of the animal's spirit: "Who knows if the spirit of man rises upward and if *the spirit of the animal* goes down into the earth?" (NIV)

With no intention of being overly critical, I believe some well-meaning Bible students handle this verse somewhat carelessly, citing the KJV translation and suggesting that this verse is contrasting an animal spirit with a human spirit. Verse 21 of the KJV reads, "Who knoweth the spirit of man that goeth upward, and the spirit of the beast that goeth downward to the earth?" Note the difference in translation compared to the NIV. With somewhat less than a careful reading these students jump to the conclusion that an animal's spirit goes "downward" into the earth. They subsequently take another unwarranted leap and reason, somehow, that since the animal's spirit goes down into the earth there is no future for an animal after physical death. But this is clearly not what the passage is saying when it is examined with attention.

Unfortunately, the KJV translation can be misleading and does not naturally fit the context as well as the NIV or several other translations for the following reasons: (1) the context is emphasizing the sameness of man's fate with the animals, not differences (vv.19, 20), (2) the use of the word "spirit" in this passage, again, relates to the breath of life which man shares with the animals (v.19), and (3) the testimony of other Bible translations also reflects the same thought as the NIV. As the Holman Bible Dictionary states, "the NIV translation better renders the thought of 3:21 than the KJV's translation." Solomon is emphasizing that death negates the differences between people and animals. In other words, the entire context is speaking of similarities, not differences.

Careful study tells us that Eccl. 3:18-21 is certainly not saying that the spirits of all animals go downward any more than it is saying that the spirits of all men go upward! Solomon is stating that no one, by comparing the carcass of an animal to a human corpse, can find evidence of where either one goes after physical death. *Nothing* in this passage teaches that the *ruach* (spirit) of the animal ceases to exist at the point of physical death! In fact, the *ruach* of man and the *ruach* of the animal are both clearly spoken of in exactly the same manner. Nevertheless, the essential point to grasp, here, is that "the spirit of the animal" is again explicitly referred to.

We know that "God gave Solomon wisdom and very great insight, and a breadth of understanding as measureless as the sand on the seashore" (1 Kings 4:29) as he "taught about animals." (v. 33) It is virtually impossible to imagine that Solomon, under the Holy Spirit's control, would use the expression "the spirit (*ruach*) of the animal" in this context if animals consisted merely of flesh and bones, particularly in view of previous discussion in this article. It is even more difficult to imagine the Holy Spirit would refer to an animal's *ruach* (spirit) relocating to some other place (v. 21) if it has ceased to exist at death!

Solomon, writing under the Holy Spirit's direction in Ecclesiastes 3:21, is speaking of the relocation of the animal *spirit* at the time of death! Ecclesiastes 3:21 should be studied carefully by the student. To summarize, we have another important passage referring to "the spirit of the animal," and this passage is consistent with the Bible's teaching in Gen. 2:7, 6:17, 7:22, Psalm 104:29, and others, providing, in connection with other passages, very strong evidence for the existence of the animal soul or spirit. The Brown-Driver-Briggs Hebrew lexicon, the standard among Old Testament Hebrew lexicons, lists as one of its primary definitions for *ruach*: "spirit of the living, breathing being in man and animals."

Although this student has very high regard for Hebrew scholars of the caliber of Gleason Archer and others, these scholars are not always correct. It was very revealing to study Archer's discourse on Ecclesiastes 3:21 in his *Encyclopedia of Bible Difficulties*. In his analysis of this verse on page 258 Archer refers to Gen. 6:17, 7:15, and 7:22 and then writes, "I am not aware of any other passage in which *ruach* is used with respect to animals." This is an amazing statement from a scholar of this caliber. Psalm 104:29 apparently completely escaped his attention! This verse is actually the most important and instructive of all Biblical references to the *ruach* of the animal, and *when translated literally* it is undoubtedly the most determinative with respect to the entire issue! As previously pointed out, this verse tells us the Lord gathers the animal's *ruach* (spirit) at the time of physical death! Archer has simply erred.

Summary

As alluded to earlier, some scholars attempt to say that the *ruach* or "spirit" in the animal is a metonymy referring merely to the immaterial consciousness and that, therefore, there is no immaterial life-element to an animal. But careful Biblical analysis supports the conclusion that the "*ruach* of the animal" is much more than a mere metonymy. In light of the foregoing discussion, the gospel account of Jesus entering into the country of the Gergesenes (Matt. 8:28-34) provides us with sufficiently clear insight into the genuine nature of God's most amazing and complex earthly creation outside the human race.

In this account Jesus sent a multitude of demons out of two men who had been powerfully energized by these unclean spirits (v. 28). He then permitted them, at their request, to enter into a herd of pigs. After carefully reading through this passage and Matt. 12:43-45, the student should ask himself this important and decisive question: Why would these unclean spirits (Mk. 5:13) desire to "enter into" a herd of pigs (Matt. 8:30-32) unless they had already identified a spiritual region within a pig's body which could be occupied by one or more spirits? Why would these spirits have any desire to enter into an animal's body if such a creature is merely a set of biochemical processes with no capacity to accommodate an immaterial spirit? The Bible is sufficiently clear, when translated normally and interpreted literally, that an animal is not merely a walking biochemical machine independent of an animating spirit.

Those familiar with the Greek text should especially note the explicit nature of the Greek in reporting that these spirits "entered *into* the pigs" (Mk. 5:13, lit.), obviously referring to entry into their bodies. From this passage it is evident that there is an invisible region or field within an animal's physical body which is capable of accommodating one or more spirits which can energize the physical body. When important passages are viewed collectively, the Bible seems to point to the fact that an animal's body will function only as it is energized by at least one immaterial spirit. In the words of the Psalmist, "You (Lord) take away their spirit, they expire and return to their dust." (Ps. 104:29 NASB) Borrowing the words of James, as he relates to the human condition, "the body without the spirit is dead." (James 2:26) It is the settled opinion of this student that the commonly held position that an animal does not "have" a soul or spirit is not derived from careful exegesis of the Word of God while comparing Scripture with Scripture.

Although it is not the intent of this author to be exhaustive, key passages in the animal soul/spirit issue give unmistakable biblical evidence for the probability of an immaterial being existing within the animal's physical body. These key passages provide abundant evidence that the classical view of the church for centuries was almost certainly correct and is also the view most clearly suggested in the Word of God. When these key passages are examined, the following summary emerges, leaving little doubt in this author's mind concerning the animating life force behind a living, breathing animal. In the words of Young's literal translation, this animating life force of an air-breathing animal appears to be that of "a living spirit." "...all in whose nostrils is breath *of a living spirit...*" (Gen. 7:22 YLT)

1. With respect to sum and substance, the terms *soul* and *spirit* are fundamentally equivalent in both the New and Old Testaments and refer to the same immaterial essence of the creature. (e.g. Isa. 26:9, Job 7:11, Luke 1:46,47) We see that *nephesh* (soul, being) and *ruach* (spirit, breath) are both used in connection with air-breathing

animals in the Old Testament.

2. *Nephesh* (Heb.) and *psuche* (Gk.), the common words for "soul" in the Old and New Testaments are used with reference to both man and animal. (Gen. 1:20, 24, 2:7, Rev. 16:3)

3. Both mankind and air-breathing animals are said to possess "the breath of the spirit (*ruach*) of life" (Gen. 7:22, NKJV, NASB), or in the words of Young's literal translation, "the breath of a living spirit (Gen. 7:22, 6:17 YLT)," referring to the immaterial essence of these creatures.

4. The physical bodies of men and animals are both said to be animated by the same life breath which comes from the Lord (Eccl. 3:19, 21, cf. Job 34:14-15, Psalm 104:29). This life-element of man or animal is said to be dependent on God's Spirit and God's breath, without which the body cannot function and returns to dust. (Job 34:15, Ps. 104:29 NASB, James 2:26, cf. Matt. 8:32).

5. The Bible clearly speaks of the *ruach* of the animal at least twice in contexts where it is almost universally translated "spirit." (Gen. 7:22, NKJV, Eccl. 3:21 NIV) This verse speaks of the "spirit of man" and "spirit of the animal." As with the case of man, there is ample reason to believe that when an animal dies "the dust will return to earth as it was, and the spirit will return to God who gave it." (cp. Eccl. 12:7 with Ps. 104:29 NASB)

6. Even when *ruach* is translated "breath" rather than "spirit," such as in Gen. 6:17, animals with nostrils are nonetheless said to possess "the breath of life." This does not, in any way, imply that animals are created in the image of God. But it does teach that animals possess a similar type of element that makes man a "living being," when we compare this expression to Genesis 2:7.

Conclusion

We see the terms *"soul"* and *"spirit"* are frequently equated in the Bible and that both are Biblically associated with the lives of air-breathing animals. Although man alone is said to be created "in the image of God," both humans and animals come from the same dust of the earth and are animated by the same source of life, the breath of God (Eccl. 3:21, cf. Job 34:14-15, Psalm 104:29 NASB). At the time of physical death, human and animal bodies both return to the same place, that is, to the dust (Ps. 104:29, Eccl. 3:18-21), while both types of spirits are said to be received by the LORD (Psalm 104:29 NASB; cf. Eccl. 12:7). There appears to be unmistakable evidence for the existence of an animal spirit in air-breathing animals when the Scripture is analyzed carefully and without bias. (Gen. 2:7, Gen. 7:22 NASB, NKJV, YLT; cf. Isa. 2:22) The concept of extinction of the animal spirit upon physical death would appear to be contradicted by both Psalm 104:29 (YLT, NASB) and Eccl. 3:21 (NIV), leaving every reason to believe that the animal spirit is left intact and reserved by the LORD after physical death.

The Dead Sea Scrolls are ancient manuscripts placed in caves in Palestine almost 2,000 years ago near the northwestern shore of the Dead Sea. A shepherd boy found them in 1947. Considered to be the greatest discovery of modern time, the scrolls include all the books of the Old Testament except Esther and are the oldest known manuscripts of any books of the Bible.

The Dead Sea Scrolls Uncovered, by Robert Eisenman and Michael Wise, includes the first translation and interpretation of fifty key documents of the 2,000-year-old *Dead Sea Scrolls* withheld for over thirty-five years. They give evidence of the immortal soul and spirit given both to man and the non-human creation as well.

The Dead Sea Scrolls Uncovered:
Your Holy Spirit
Fragment 9 Column 2, Fragment 10 Column 1 *(1) He (God) opened His Mercies...all the needs of His storehouse, and gave sustenance (2) to every living thing. There is none...{If he} closes his hand, and the Spi{rit of all} (3) flesh is withdrawn.* God gives life to every living thing/spirit but when He chooses, He takes their spirit back, withdraws it.

Fragment 9 Column 2, Fragment 10, referring to the spirit of all flesh reads much like Psalms 104 25-32: *There before me lies the mighty ocean, teeming with life of every kind, both great and small. And look! See the ships! And over there, the whale you made to play in the sea. Every one of these depends on you to give them daily food. You supply it, and they gather it. You open wide your hand to feed them and they are satisfied with all your bountiful provision. But if you turn away from them, then all is lost. And when you gather up their breath (spirit), they die and turn again to dust. Then you send your Spirit, and new life is born to replenish all the living of the earth. Praise God forever! How he must rejoice in all his work! The earth trembles at his glance; the mountains burst into flame at his touch.* (Psalms 104:25-32 TLB) When God gathers up or takes back their spirits, their flesh returns to dust.

And all flesh perished that moved upon the earth, both fowl, and cattle, and beast, and every swarming thing that swarmeth upon the earth, and every man; all in whose nostrils was the breath of the spirit of life, whatsoever was in the dry land, died. (Genesis 7:21-22 Holy Scriptures)

And they fell upon their faces, and said, O God, the God of the spirits of all flesh, shall one man sin, and wilt thou be wroth with all the congregation. (Numbers 16:22 KJV) These are three of the scriptures mentioned in various books of the Bible referring to the spirit of the animals.

Who knoweth not in all these that the hand of the Lord hath wrought this? In whose hand is the soul of every living thing, and the breath (spirit) of all mankind. (Job 12:9-10 KJV)

"And to every beast of the earth, and to every fowl of the air, and to every thing that creepeth upon the earth, wherein there is a living soul, [I have given] every green herb for food." And it was so. (Genesis 1:30 Holy Scriptures)

(3) Every moving thing that liveth shall be for food for you; as the green herb have I given you all. (4) Only flesh with life thereof, which is the blood thereof, shall ye not eat." (Genesis 9:3-4 Holy Scriptures) In his writing Josephus stated that the blood of animals was forbidden to be eaten, as having in it soul and spirit (Antiq. 3:11.2.) Moses set up

rules for the tribe of Levi stating what they could and could not eat. He entirely forbade them the use of blood for food, and esteemed it to contain the soul and spirit. [Eating meat with the life-blood (spirit and soul) of the animals in it is a sin. — MBP]

But if you turn away from them, then all is lost. And when you gather up their breath, (spirit) they die and turn again to dust. Then you send your Spirit, and new life is born to replenish all the living of the earth. Praise God forever! How he must rejoice in all his works! (Psalm 104:29-31 TLB) When God gathers up their spirit they die and their bodies turn to the dust. Then God sends His spirit, creating a new eternal being of both man and animals and new life/flesh is born to replenish the earth.

"For the soul of every living thing is in the hand of God, and the breath of all mankind. (Job 12:10 TLB) In this verse some would like to claim that the animal having a soul here means they don't have a spirit. There is nothing in this Scripture to indicate that they do not also have a spirit and an eternal spirit, anymore than that man does not have a soul.

After this God looked upon the earth, and filled it with his goods. The soul of every living thing hath shown forth before the face thereof, and into it they return again. (Ecclesiastes 16:30-31 HTV)

In another scripture concerning the soul we read: *"And the second angel poured out his vial upon the sea; and it became as the blood of a dead man: and every living soul died in the sea."* (Revelation 16:3 KJV) One could not interpret "soul" in this verse to mean man living in the sea and one could not interpret the souls living in the sea to simply cease to exist based on the fact that they are animals. Souls like all created entities, man and animals do not cease to exist unless willed by God and He said He created everything to live forever. Even the flesh changes form but it does not become non-existent. And a spirit being which every creature is, man, angels, animals, demons, and according to the study of plants, they even possess, remains an eternal entity.

Much is argued concerning the soul and spirit of animals and the

Holy Spirit given to redeemed man. Scripture, however, is clear that the lower animals will be restored to God according to the Bible whether one wants to deliberate the status of an animal's soul and/or spirit as we understand soul and spirit to mean. We can not claim or deny that animals have a soul and spirit any more than we can claim or deny one for ourselves as the Bible says man and beasts have both. They are mentioned in the same manner, together often within scriptures such as Psalms, Numbers Genesis, and Revelations.

The spirit of animals is mentioned in Ecclesiastes 3:21, but what confusion it has caused so many. Ray Stedman calls the Book of Ecclesiastes *The Inspired Book of Error.*

Solomon's other writings reflect God's view and not man's. The Book of Proverbs and Song of Solomon, and, many believe, The Book of Wisdom was written at least in part by Solomon as well. It is very clear that all these are truly God-inspired and written from His point of view. Compared to these books, the Book of Ecclesiastes is very humanistic. It, unlike all other books of the Bible, reflects a human rather than a divine point of view. That does not mean, however, that it is not divinely inspired. Solomon, the man known as the most wise of all men, was no doubt inspired by God to let man see the error in humanistic thinking.Ecclesiastes teases and questions. It muses and suggests; it condemns the vain thoughts of man regarding himself and creation as well. How could one, reading Ecclesiastes 3:21, even suggest that all human spirits go upward to heaven and all animal spirits go into the ground, or hell?

Theologians agree that the Book of Ecclesiastes is the most misused book of the Bible because it is written from the human rather than divine view, allowing one to quote it to prove false ideas. However, this false message is revealed within the Bible so the Bible itself reveals the errors. The Bible always points out the error that it presents and makes it clear that it is in error. Because of its humanistic character, Ecclesiastes is used by atheists, agnostics, and cults to discredit Biblical truths.

[Unfortunately many Christians as well have misused the Book of Ecclesiastes in much the same way, especially when it comes to the understanding of the spirit and eternal destination of man and animals. — MBP]

Ecclesiastes 3:21 is one of the most misunderstood and controversial Scriptures in the Bible. The things of God are the only things of value is the theme Solomon wants to impart to the reader; wealth, or lack thereof, is not important. No doubt Solomon wanted us to seek the wisdom of God and understand our purpose and the purpose of creation from the point of view of God, His word, and not man's vain pride. *Who knows whether or if,* [or *that* (depending on the Bible version*)] the spirit of man goes upward and the spirit of the animals goes downward.* (Ecclesiastes 3:21)

People generally respond in three ways when they read this verse: One, animals' spirits go down into the ground; second, animal's spirits go to heaven due to their innocent nature; third, animals have no spirit.

1. To propose that animals go into the ground, their spirits go to hell or downward and the spirits of all of mankind go to heaven is opposed to Scripture. One could not assume they cease to exist, as there is no mention in Scriptures of the spirits or souls of man, the angels, demons, or animals ceasing to exist. They go either to heaven or hell. The Old and New Testament books tell us that unrepentant man goes to hell. The scriptures indicate that the spirits of the lower animals and redeemed of mankind return to God when their bodies die (Psalm 104:1-31, etc.). The Old Testament says: *Then Ezra prayed, "You alone are God. You have made the skies and the heavens, the earth and the seas, and everything in them. You preserve it all; and all the angels of heaven worship you.* (Nehemiah 9:6 TLB) God preserveth all, both man and beast. "Preserveth" means "to keep alive, to retain, to make lasting."

2. The second belief concerning the eternal life of animals is that animals have a spirit and go to heaven because they are sinless. God

created everything to live forever in the Garden of Eden, so we can have assurance that their lives continue just as that of man. Romans 8:19-23 reminds us that the remainder of creation awaits the sons of God to be redeemed for eternal life for their new physical restoration as well. Psalms 104:29-31 speaks of the spirit of animals going back to God. Revelation 5:6-14 and Psalm 148:1-14 address the entire creation and says that the heavens, angels, hosts (all creatures), beasts, creeping things, cattle, flying fowl, and man *[Let them] praise the LORD for he commanded, and they were created. He hath also established them for ever and ever; he hath made a decree, which shall not pass.* (Psalm 148:5-6 KJV) Job 12:10 and Revelation 5, as well as many other Scriptures, give us true confidence that animals praise God for all eternity and will be in heaven.

3. The third comment made is that animals have no spirit. This has to be the most absurd comment one could make. If animals do not have a spirit, why is there any debate concerning Ecclesiastes 3:21, and why are animal spirits mentioned in the Book of Genesis (original translations), Numbers, and Psalms? There are some who recognize that animals have a spirit, yet argue that their spirits are not eternal. There is no suggestion of such a possibility in the Bible unless one interprets Ecclesiastes 3:21 in that frame of mind. *The Dead Sea Scrolls Uncovered* is the earliest recorded records of the Bible. It is impossible to deny their truth if one is to believe in the Bible. Romans 8:19-21 reflects this scroll.

The Dead Sea Scrolls Uncovered
The Splendor of the Spirits

Manuscript B Fragment 1: *(9) and all the servants of Ho{liness...} (10) in the Perfection of th{eir} works... (11) in {their} wond{rous} Temples...(12) {a}ll {their} servant{s ...} (13) Your Holiness in the habitat{ion of...}* Fragment 2 *(1)...them, and they shall bless Your Holy Name with blessing{s}...(2) and they shall bless} You, all creatures of flesh in unison, whom {You} have creat{ed...(3) be}asts and birds and reptiles and the fish of the seas, and all...(4) {Y}ou have created them all anew...* Fragment 3

(13*)... The Holy Spirit {sett}led upon His Messiah...*

Ecclesiastes 3:11 warns us of the lack of knowledge and under-standing of mankind concerning the remainder of creation, as Solomon explains. *Everything is appropriate in its own time. But though God has planted eternity in the hearts of men, even so, man cannot see the whole scope of God's work* (creation) *from beginning to end.* (Ecclesiastes 3:11 TLB)

In his commentary on Ecclesiastes 1 through 3, Matthew Henry states, "They are all meaningless. 2. Everything is meaningless, not only in the abuse of it, when it is perverted by the sin of man, but even in the use of it. It is expressed here very emphatically; not only, all is vain, but in the abstract, all is meaningless; as if meaninglessness were the proprium quarto mode-property in the fourth mode, of the things of this world, that which enters into the nature of them. They are not only meaningless, but utterly meaningless, the vainest meaningless-ness, meaningless in the highest degree." Relate the commentary of Matthew Henry with Romans 8:19, as all is futile, vain, and useless for both man and beast.

[Ecclesiastes 3:15 says that what God created was, is, and will be. He destroys nothing in creation. It has continuation whether we are speaking about the non-human creatures or mankind. God gave us a choice being created in His image and higher than the lower animals, yet lower than the angels. Unlike the animals and little children, and some mentally challenged, we come to an age when we know that we have to choose God or Satan. — MBP]

That which has been made, the same continueth: the things that shall be, have already been: and God restoreth that which is past. (Ecclesiastes 3:15 Douay Rheims Bible)

In the explanation in the footnotes from the New American Bible, the interpretation of 3:15: "God restores: the meaning is probably that God allows no part of his creation to drop out of existence."

That which hath been is now; and that which is to be hath already been; and God requireth that which is past. (Ecclesiastes 3:15 KJV)

That which is hath been long ago, and that which is to be hath already been; and God seeketh that which is pursued. (Ecclesiastes 3:15 Holy Scriptures)

Whatever is has already been. The world, as it has been, is and will be constant in constancy; for God will call the past to account, that is, repeats what he has formerly done. There has no change befallen us, but such as is common to men. (Ecclesiastes 3:15 Matthew Henry Commentary)

All go unto one place; all are of the dust, and all return to dust. Who knoweth the spirit of man whether it goeth upward, and the spirit of the beast whether it goeth downward to the earth? (Ecclesiastes 3:20-21 Holy Scriptures)

The world or creation will be restored. It will return to its pure and perfect form before man contaminated the creation through disobedience to God.

When the King James Version was translated to English, the translator changed the word "soul" when referring to animals as "living being or being." After that time other editions of the Bible followed suit. The word "that" within Ecclesiastes 3:21 confuses some readers as it gives an impression that animals' spirits went downward. In Ecclesiastes 3:21 of the King James Version concerning animal spirits we read: *Who knoweth the spirit of man that goeth upward, and the spirit of the beast that goeth downward to the earth?* And though the word "spirit" was left referring to animals, the word "if" (sometimes translated "whether") was changed to "that," leading the reader of the King James Version to believe that animals' spirits go down into the earth, or to hell. Ecclesiastes 3:21 is a question, not a statement of fact. This should be a red flag that Solomon was not making a statement of fact. Nonetheless, it has caused much confusion among many who had not understood this statement of Solomon.

And the dust returns to the ground as it was, and the life breath returns to God who bestowed it. Utter futility—said Koheleth—All is futile! (Ecclesiastes 12:7-8, Kethuvim-The Jewish Bible)

Who knows if a man's life breath does rise upward and if a beast's breath does sink down into the earth? I saw that there is nothing better for man than to enjoy his possessions, since that is his portion. For who can enable him to see what will happen afterward? (Ecclesiastes 3:21-22 Kethuvim–The Jewish Bible)

Who knoweth the spirit of the children of men? Doth it go upwards? And the spirit of the beasts, doth it go downwards to the earth? (Ecclesiastes 3:21, The Darby Bible)

We have to determine if all of the children of Adam, everyone who has ever lived, is going to heaven. We know according to the Bible that all of the children of Adam are not going to heaven. So, how could anyone assume the spirits of the animals are going into the earth or hell?

Ecclesiastes 3:15 says all continue on. This is the eternal continuing of all created spirits and souls of flesh including both man and beast. *The Lord is gracious, and full of compassion; slow to anger and of great mercy. The Lord is good to all; and His tender mercies are over all His works. All Thy works shall praise Thee, O Lord; And Thy saints shall bless Thee. The Lord preserveth all them that love Him; But all the wicked will He destroy. My mouth shall speak the praise of the Lord; and let all flesh bless His holy name for ever and ever.* (Psalm 145:8-10, 21-22 Holy Scriptures) All thy works shall praise thee, (all the animals) and all "Saints" (God's children), those redeemed of mankind, and all non-human creation will praise His Holy name forever.

In Psalm 145:20 and 21, God is preserving all that love Him. He is destroying all that do not love Him. We would not surmise from that statement that all that hate God, He will eliminate from existence forever. They will be going where love is completely void. But all that love Him he is preserving in heaven. Psalm 145 says that the animals, all thy works/creation, praise Him. Is that not a form of love and admiration? And since all flesh will bless His holy name for ever and ever it would include the animal kingdom as well as mankind.

He hath made all things good in their time, and hath delivered the world to their consideration, so that man can not find out the work, which

God hath made from the beginning to the end. And I have known that there was no better thing than to rejoice, and to do well in this life. For every man that eateth and drinketh, and seeth good of his labor, this is the gift of God. I have learned that all the works which God hath made, continue for ever: we cannot add any thing, nor take away from those things which God hath made that he may be feared. That which hath been made, the same continueth: the things that shall be, have already been: and God restoreth that which is past. I saw under the sun in the place of judgment wickedness, and in the place of justice iniquity. And I said in my heart: God shall judge both the just and the wicked, and then shall be the time of every thing. I said in my heart concerning the sons of men, that God would prove then, and shew them to be like beasts. Therefore the death of man and of beasts is one, and the condition of them both is equal: as man dieth, so they also die: all things breathe alike, and man hath nothing more than beast: all things are subject to vanity. And all things go to one place: of earth they were made, and into earth they return together. Who knoweth if the spirits of the children of Adam ascend upward, and if the spirit of the beasts descends downward? (Ecclesiastes 3:11-21 Douay Rheims Bible)

In verses 15 and 17 in the Douay Rheims Old Testament, dating back to the early 1600s, it states that all things continue forever, which aligns with Romans 8:21, which states the time to come "that all creation awaits the children of God to be revealed." Notice the word "vanity": *All is vanity for both man and animals as mentioned for the creature was made subject to vanity, not willingly, but by reason of him who hath subjected the same in hope.* (Romans 8:19-21 KJV) The "creature" here is referring to the remainder of creation, not the creature man as Leon Morris relates in his book, *The Cross of Jesus.* He states: "Some scholars see a reference to mankind in these words. But it is hard to believe that this was Paul's meaning. He cannot be referring to the regenerate, for he differentiates the saved from 'the whole creation.' Nor can he mean the unregenerate, for he does not regard them as being brought into the liberty of the glory of the sons of God. It is unlikely that the words refer to good angels, for they were not subjected to the futility of which Paul writes, or to evil angels, for they are not looking forward to the revelation of the sons of God. Paul is surely referring to the whole creation below the personal level; he is speaking of animals and birds and trees, and flowers."

[No person of reason could assume that mankind would go to heaven and the animal kingdom would go to hell or cease to exist. Would a loving God send the innocent of creation that have suffered the most and sacrificed their lives for man go to hell or non-existence? That is man's vain doctrine. It is not of God. God says He has mercy for all His creation. If you were God and created all of the creatures of the world, would you send them all to non-existence or to hell? Every time I hear people react as if offended by the thought that animals go to heaven, I can't help but think how selfish and cruel their hearts are and how much it hurts our heavenly father. — MBP]

Solomon knew what the prophets and Old Testament writers including David, Solomon's father, said about the souls and spirits of the animals, God's eternal covenant with them, their praises to God and His provisions and preservation of creation stated throughout Scripture.

God made a covenant with Noah and the animals. He revealed that each type of animal possesses a soul. God made an eternal covenant with man and the animals. God made the eternal covenant with Noah (Noe), his family, and referred to the souls of all of the animals. *And God spake unto Noah (Noe), and to his sons with him, saying, And I, behold, I establish my covenant with you, and with your seed after you; And with every living soul that is with you as well in all birds as in cattle and beasts of the earth, that are come forth out of the ark, and in all the beasts of the earth. ... And God said: This is the sign of the covenant which I give between me and you, and every living soul that is with you, for perpetual generations. And the bow shall be in the clouds, and I shall see it, and shall remember the everlasting covenant, that was made between God and every living soul of all flesh which is upon the earth.* (Genesis 9:8-17 Douay Rheims Bible)

Then God said to Noah (Noe) and to his sons with him, "I will establish my covenant with you, and with your descendants after you; and with every living creature that is with you, the birds, the cattle, and every wild animal with you; all that came out of the ark, even the wild animals. I establish my covenant with you. Never again shall all flesh be destroyed by the waters of the flood; never again shall there be a flood to destroy the earth. And God said, "This is the token of the covenant; I set it between me and you and every living creature that is with you, for all generations to come. (Genesis 9:8-17 St. Joseph New Catholic Edition).

Seven times within ten verses, Moses, in the Book of Genesis, speaks of God as establishing a covenant with all flesh and with every living soul. It is an everlasting covenant that He will not destroy the earth again with water. Why was it so important to mention the animals so often within those ten verses as not only having souls, but that God had established a covenant with them also? If they were not to know of anything beyond this life, if there was no reason for such a promise of the future, if animals are simply only mortal, irrational, brainless, animated beings, why did God repeatedly make such a point of an everlasting covenant with them? In his letters to the various churches mentioned in the Bible, Paul tells us Jesus is restoring all creation back to God just as John wrote of in Revelation 5:6-14.

CHAPTER 3

The Wisdom and Intelligence of Man and Animals

St. Bonaventure:

"The creatures of the sense world signify the invisible attributes of God, partly because God is the origin, exemplar and end of every creature, and every effect is the sign of its cause, the exemplification of its exemplar and the path to the end, to which it leads...For every creature is by its nature a kind of effigy and likeness of the eternal Wisdom. Therefore, open your eyes, alert the ears of your spirit open your lips and apply your heart so that in all creatures you may see, hear, praise, love and worship, glorify and honor your God."

References:

- *Reader's Digest Marvels and Mysteries of Our Animal World*
- David Hume, *Treatise of Human Nature*
- Adam Smith, *Theory of Moral Sentiments*
- David Hartley, *Observations on Man: His Frame, His Duty, and His Expectations*

1 Kings speaks of Solomon seeking and receiving wisdom even to the extent of wisdom concerning the animals. We are always to seek wisdom just as Solomon did, and God will give us His wisdom. Solomon was very young when he became king and he learned from his father David the value of being honest and fair in the treatment of those under his kingship. Above all, he asked God to guide him in this manner. The Lord was pleased that Solomon had asked for this and so he said to him, *Because you have asked for the wisdom to rule justly instead of long life for yourself or riches or death of your enemies, I will do what you have asked. I will give you more wisdom and understanding than anyone has ever had before or will ever have again. And he spoke three thousand proverbs; and his songs were a thousand and five. And he spoke of trees, from the cedar that is in Lebanon even unto the hyssop that springeth out of the wall; he spoke also of beasts, and of fowl, and of creeping things, and of fishes.* (1 Kings 5:9, 12-13, Holy Scriptures)

Wisdom and intelligence are found to some degree in all of God's creatures, according to Solomon. The Book of Wisdom denotes eternal life. *Having meditated on all this, and having come to the conclusion that immortality resided in kinship with Wisdom—but, realizing that I could never possess Wisdom unless God gave her to me, a sign of intelligence in itself, to know in whose gift she lay—I prayed to the Lord and entreated him, and with all my heart I said,* (Wisdom 8:17,21 NJV) *God of our ancestors, Lord of mercy, who by your word have made the universe, and in your wisdom have fitted human beings to rule the creatures that you have made, to govern the world in holiness and saving justice and in honesty of soul to dispense fair judgment, and grant me Wisdom, consort of your throne, and do not reject me from the number of your children.* (Wisdom 9:1-4 NJV)

All wisdom comes from the Lord; she is with him forever. The sands of the sea, the drops of rain, the days of eternity—who can count them? The height of the sky, the breadth of the earth, the depth of the abyss—who can explore them? Wisdom was created before everything; prudent understanding subsists from remotest ages. For whom has the root of wisdom ever been uncovered? Her resourceful ways, who knows them? One only is wise; terrible indeed, seated on his throne, the Lord. It was he who created, inspected and weighed her up, and then poured her out on all his works—as much to each living creature as he chose—bestowing her on those who love him. (Ecclesiasticus 1: 1-10 NJV)

Wisdom 8:17 speaks of the sign of intelligence being part of immortality. In verse 21, Wisdom is a sign of intelligence and in

Ecclesiasticus 1:9-10, continuing on with Wisdom, God gave wisdom to all His works, each living creature/all creation—not just man, but every living creature.

In these scriptures we find that wisdom is in all things innocent, of God both the upright of man and the non-human creation and they are part of God's army in defeating the wicked once and for all. *For Wisdom is quicker to move than any motion; she is so pure, she pervades and permeates all things. She is a breath of the power of God, pure emanation of the glory of the Almighty; so nothing impure can find its way into her.* (Wisdom 7:24 NJV) *For light must yield to night, but against Wisdom evil can not prevail. Strongly she reaches from one end of the world to the other and she governs the whole world for its good.* (Wisdom 7:30 NJV) *For the creation, being at the service of you, its Creator tautens to punish the wicked and slackens for the benefit of those who trust in you.* (Wisdom 16:24 NJV) *Who endowed the ibis with wisdom and gave the cock his intelligence?* (Job 38:36 NJV)

Solomon speaks of some of the smallest of creation and their wisdom. *There are four things which are little upon the earth, But they are exceeding wise: The ants are a people not strong, Yet they provide their food in the summer; The rock-badgers are but a feeble folk, Yet make they their houses in the crags; The locusts have no king, Yet go they forth all of them by bands; The spider thou canst take with the hands, Yet is she in kings' palaces.* (Proverbs 30:24-28, Holy Scriptures)

Even birds and animals have much they could teach you; ask the creatures of earth and sea for this wisdom. All of them know that the LORD'S hand made them. It is God who directs the lives of his creatures; every man's life is in his power. (Job 12:7-10 Good News Bible)

Who has made us more intelligent than wild animals, wiser than birds in the skies? (Job 35:11 NJV)

Stupid men will start being wise when wild donkeys are born tame. (Job 11:12, Good News Bible) Scripture tells man to seek wisdom through the lives and work ethics of His lesser creatures.

Wisdom will never enter the soul of a wrong-doer, nor dwell in a body enslaved to sin; for the holy spirit of instruction flees deceitfulness, recoils from unintelligent thoughts, is thwarted by the onset of vice. (Wisdom 1:4-5 NJV)

The Bible also speaks of the intelligence and spiritual awareness of the donkey of Balaam in Numbers 22:20-33, Jonah 2:1-2, 10, Proverbs 30:24-28 and other scriptures.

Do animals really have the ability to reason?

A rational soul has the heart, mind, ability to reason and make decisions. This intelligence, God-given gift, wisdom, is apparent in many animals, such as dogs, as they often make decisions at high levels. Their intelligence to know what to do to save lives and help those with various types of physical and mental limitation, such as the blind, is found in their ability to learn many tasks. Their soul/mind, however, is different from that of man, as they do not have the free will to choose between God and Satan. Man was given a free will, as were the angels; however, the angels do not have the right to choose. So in viewing the relationship of each type of the three beings, having or not having a free will does not determine that any of the three types do or do not possess high intelligence or that they do or do not go to heaven. The animals were subjected to man's free will, and under his control while on earth. No infant or mentally challenged person can make the decision to accept salvation or reject it. Does one then believe that they do not go to heaven? The animals in their altered nature due to man's sins are or are not obedient to man. Whether that is to act with kindness and forgiveness toward man or in evil ways as put in their hearts by God for self survival as He said He would put a fear of man in their hearts/souls as stated in Genesis. As for all creatures, though they have been put in subjection to man on earth, their spirits remain innocent, and upon physical death, they, through the sacrifice of Jesus, together with the redeemed of mankind, are restored to God.

Can animals learn through trial and error? Our crow learned through trial and error after two attempts to hide a button under a rug. He pulled the rug back with his beak, let go and took the button to place it where the upturned rug was but the rug had flopped back over so he could not hide it. He then attempted this again, but the third time, he put his foot on the upturned rug while holding the corner of the rug in his mouth. He then let go of the rug with his beak, picked up the button and placed it neatly under where the rug would be when he released his foot. It worked, and he strolled off across the living room floor, proud that he had accomplished his desired goal.

Could a crow accomplish more complex tasks? A televised *National Geographic* special used mental mapping to see if crows and ravens could figure out how to get something they wanted by following a specific string. A fish was placed in a hole tied to a string. The bird immediately figured out that by pulling the fish up by the string as far as it could pull with its beak, then, while holding the string in its mouth, place its foot on the string, release the string out of its mouth and grabbing hold of the string farther down in the hole and pulling it up repeating the same process, it could finally get hold of the fish. For a more advanced test, the experimenters tied a piece of meat up in a tree on the end of the string but also had another string with a rock on its end criss-crossing over the one with the meat. The crow instantly knew which string to pull on to get the meat.

Can crows use tools? *National Geographic* discovered that crows and primates as well as dolphins use tools very well. The crows find twigs that will get the grubs, which are in rocks, out to eat by selecting the perfect sticks. They grab one end of the stick with their beak and push the other end of the stick into the crack of the rock and stick the grub with it, then pull the stick back out with the grub firmly attached.

Henry Ward Beecher said the common crow is a feathered genius and an endlessly astonishing bird. Some mimic what a person says; they mimic dogs' barks, cats' meows, and other birds as well.

They love to play tricks on other crows by stealing their neighbor's nesting material and when they leave their nest, the neighbor comes and takes it back with a little additional choice material besides.

I grew up on a farm and watched as my brother Mac Allen attempted to hunt crows from time to time. We could never figure out how they could tell when a person is carrying a gun rather than a fishing pole or some other object. I was to learn that crows actually have one of their kind posted in a tree, and when a person comes within a quarter mile of view with a gun they have a very distinctive call that alerts the others and they all fly off to safety at about 45 miles an hour. They have great eyesight, as do many birds.

The honey bee knows without being taught how to build using the least amount of wax a cell that will hold the largest possible amount of honey. The hexagonal cell is of such perfect geometrical measurements that men can not improve upon it, yet the bees, untaught, working in co-operation with a multitude of other bees, build a perfect cell in the dark.

Elephants have behavior much like that of a person. Their emotions seem as strong of those of mankind and their care for the young is most compassionate. In *Reader's Digest Marvels and Mysteries of Our Animal World* (1964), Bill Ryan, who studied elephants for more than forty years, reported that at one of the camps a herd of elephants used to raid the garden. They tried putting a fence up but the elephants just trampled it down so they installed a fence with a generator and electrified it. Within a few nights the elephants had figured out that when the lights went out the electric fence would not shock them so down the fence went again. But if they kept the generator running all night surely the big beasts would finally give up. No, that was not to happen either. The elephants came back poking on the wires until one of them found that his tusks were nonconductive. As a last resort, rangers had to stand guard at night using shotguns to frighten them away.

A young elephant mother-to-be will seek the company of an older cow that will stay with her after the calf is born and help protect it from any harm. The older cow may also assist in the birth, and other females as well if needed.

There is great affection exchanged between the mother and calf, and when a youngster gets out of line the mother disciplines her young calf. When the calf does get into serious trouble, other elephants will come to the rescue. A calf was walking too close to the edge of a bank when the earth gave way and it fell into the water. The cows tried to get the youngster to take their trunks as they reached out for it, but it was too scared to know what to do, so two cows knelt on the bank while the other two lowered themselves carefully into the water. Between them making encouraging sounds to the waterlogged, coughing calf, the latter two put their tusks under him and lifted him high enough for the two on the bank to get hold of him and pull him to safety. The youngster, nervous and scared, cuddled up to his mother, who, showing great compassion, checked him out with her trunk by feeling all over him. But, after deciding he was not injured in any way, she sternly disciplined him by giving him a very hard wallop with her trunk. Then, screeching in anger at the top of her lungs, chased him away from the water's edge.

While warden at Murchison Falls National Park, Colonel C.D. Trimmer experienced the grief of a mother elephant over her dead calf. He observed that for three days the mother carried the little carcass, laying it on the ground only when she had to get a drink. Later he found her standing beside a tree but there was no calf. She stayed there for several days in mourning without food and would not allow anyone to come near. Several days later she left, and when Trimmer went to the site he found that she had dug a grave under the tree and buried her calf there.

Elephants are often used for moving logs. They are more highly regarded than horses, as they are much stronger and can move with ease through the forests. They are very agile, which helps greatly traveling through the forest. There has been at least one tribe of people in India who have trained their elephants to work five days a week, but when the weekend comes the elephants head for quite some distance to the water where they swim and play all weekend; yet faithfully, every Monday morning, they are back at the camp ready to work. They do this without human intervention in any way.

When injured, elephants also will allow man to treat them and they learn by scent a man who hunts with a gun and one who is their friend. An old bull that can no longer keep up with the herd is often spotted with two young males who stay with him to protect him until he dies. Elephants live to be about sixty if allowed to live out their life.

Wild orangutans that lived near a camp showed up and helped share the chores they saw the people doing, such as washing laundry in the river, rinsing and wringing it out.

John and Michele Helfrich of Justin, Texas, had a bovine longhorn calf named Beanie that watched John repair a water line that had sprung a leak. To repair the pipe he first had to dig a trench on both sides of the pipe. The heifer stood beside him the entire day, observing his actions. Then, to his amazement, when he started filling the trench back in, she would stand beside him and push the dirt in. Finally, he jumped in the trench, and when he did, Beanie jumped in with him and started stomping the dirt down. When he got back out to shove more dirt in, she would get out and push the dirt with her head. The ditch was five feet deep, and when she jumped in and out, she really had to jump.

Can dolphins imitate actions immediately? Again, the *National Geographic* team did flips in the water and used various devices in the water, and immediately the dolphins would do the very same thing on the first try.

Pigeons can identify shapes and know the difference between large and small areas. Chimps demonstrate abstract thinking abilities. They can push the numbers on a kind of calculator and identify the numbers they see on a screen in front of them.

Parrots can identify numbers in the same way the chimps do and they can also vocalize the numbers. They can count as well. In fact, parrots can vocalize almost as many words as people can.

Chickens give specific calls for different predators. Dogs can understand physical language in communicating with man. Dolphins can grasp complete sentences and then follow directions accurately.

There have been so many experiments backed up by the Bible that animals have intelligence, can reason, and make decisions. They do to some degree also possess wisdom given by God. The many aspects of the understanding of creation below man are all intertwined through the Hand of God. It would be the folly of man to reject God's word. Experiments and common observations have demonstrated that animals have deep emotional levels, feel pain, mourn the loss of both their animal companions and human companions as well.

James Burgh, a Scottish moralist of the 1700s, found that God wills the happiness of all rational creatures; and he admitted that animals show "signs of reflection, gratitude, and faithfulness: and a sort of rationality as well. He left the impression that God, willing good to all reflective things, must, by the very resemblance between beasts and men, have an interest in both.

Philosopher David Hume came from Scotland and was influenced by Calvinistic doctrine, though later his approach to religion changed drastically. He did not believe in miracles or ministries that proclaimed miracles. Yet his belief in the understanding of the intelligence of creation was quite forward thinking. In 1739 he discussed animal sympathy in his anonymously published *Treatise of Human Nature*. He said, "Although beasts have no feeling for kinship, they do have a strong feeling of acquaintanceship and a love of kind. Through a crowd of people or a herd of cattle, anger and fear pass with lightning swiftness. Grief likewise is received by sympathy; and produces almost all the same consequences, and excites the same emotions as in our species." Animals play as they fight, a dog with his teeth, a lion with his paws. "Yet they most carefully avoid harming their companion, even though they have nothing to fear from his resentment; which is an evident proof of the sense brutes have of each other's pain and pleasure."

In 1759 Adam Smith stated in *Theory of Moral Sentiments* that sympathy is the fundamental fact of moral consciousness. It is impossible to conceive of a sensitive and innocent being, high or low, human or otherwise, whose happiness we should not desire. Our kindly feelings of the lowest animals are proportionally low; but they rise as we consider those nearest ourselves and reach the highest point of all as we look to our own species.

David Hartley was the son of an Anglican clergyman living near Halifax, Yorkshire. He became a medical doctor and engaged in mathematical research. His theological concepts were in conflict with the Church of England. His ideas caused much support and yet much dissent. He wrote *Observations on Man: His Frame, His Duty, and His Expectations* in 1749 stating: "Science has lately shown us that even seemingly inanimate things show signs of life like ours, and this is argument enough for a greater consideration of their pleasure and pain." Animals are also like us in "the formation of their intellects, memories, and passions, and in the signs of distress, fear, pain and death. They often likewise win our affections by the marks of peculiar mental discernment or soundness of judgement, their instincts, helplessness, innocence, and benevolence."

CHAPTER 4

Merciful God, Merciless Man

References:

- The Very Rev. James E. Carroll, Commentary on *Merciful God, Merciless Man*
- Pope John Paul II, *Crossing the Threshold of Hope*
- Matthew Henry, *Commentary*
- Dix Harwood, *Love for Animals*
- Rev. Dr. Dewitt Talmage, Presbyterian Minister, *Sermons from 1869 to 1902*
- Rev. John Hildrop

*T*he view of true Christians concerning the treatment of animals is beautifully expressed by Reverend James E. Carroll, an Episcopal priest in San Diego, California. Reverend Carroll delivered a sermon he gave me permission to quote: "The Church of God is concerned with all life, when she is true to the Divine vocation, and thus 'all' includes the creatures of God's animal kingdom...

"The callous may escape the prosecution of human law, but he will never escape divine judgment, for he has abused the dominion which God gave him over the creatures, and there are few graver sins than this"...

"A committed Christian, who knows what his religion is about, will never kill an animal needlessly. Above all, he will do his utmost to put a stop to any kind of cruelty to any animal. A Christian who participates in or gives consent to cruelty to animals had better reexamine his religion or else drop the name Christian."

In the Jewish tradition of Jesus' time, animals, especially livestock, were to be treated humanely. Man was to care for them and

49

keep them from suffering. They were considered part of the household and were not to be exploited for man's benefit.

Archbishop York and Roman Catholic Cardinal Manning joined the Victoria Street Society in London to regulate vivisection and bring about its abolishment in 1875. About fifty years earlier, in 1824, the Royal Society for the Protection of Animals was founded by Reverend Arthur Boome, a Christian minister. And even earlier, Reverend Dr. Humphry Primatt published the book *The Duty of Mercy and the Sin of Cruelty to Brute Animals* in 1776. Yet even with the founding of societies and books written to protect animals and bring understanding of the humane way animals were to be treated and the Christian's duty to uphold the rights or humane treatment of animals, the establishment of laboratories to perform vivisection on innocent animals keeps growing with no regard to the torture and pain inflicted upon the animals in the name of science.

[Vivisection means the cutting open and torturing of live animals, usually without any anesthetic or means to reduce or eliminate pain endured by the animal, in the name of science. This totally unmerciful and cruel treatment began long ago and is still prevalent in most of the countries of the world today, including the United States. This type of needless torture and abuse is going on in universities, experimental labs, and other institutions of learning and research experimentation throughout the country. Millions of these animals are dogs and cats. Even human slaves have been used. The acceptance of this practice hinges on the belief that animals do not feel pain, do not have emotions and do not have a soul or spirit; therefore, they are simply animated objects, even though the cruel and godless perpetrator sees the animals crying out in pain, and flinch when inflicted with knives. The fact that supposedly great scientists are doing this, believing that the animals have no feelings or purpose other than that for which man chooses to use them, is most frightening, and to those who have godly wisdom and a logical ability of reasoning know to be completely untrue. If one cannot observe and hear and see the pain of innocent creatures as they are butchered, one will not hear the cry or see the worth of humans either, other than themselves. They are not people of wisdom. They lack true understanding. The fact that they cannot see nor hear any pain from those innocent creatures has to indicate that they do not have in a true sense a soul, as we know it, of God. We have seen the evidence and heard the horrors of the Holocaust. We know that no God would be behind this type of torture and death and we know that our Heavenly Father is a merciful God. God is devastated due to the pain and heartbreak of our earthly acts of evil upon man and animals alike. It is not what a person says about how much they love and praise God; the evidence is in the way they treat all creation, and praise God for all He has given us in nature to love and care for. Man so often fakes true beliefs and feelings to others. How interesting that animals though they do vocalize in their own languages, yet in this present world can not communicate in a way we can in most cases understand, do not fake their love or fear of us in ways we can understand. They either respond with fear or suspicion toward man or in complete love. — MBP]

The Catechism of the Catholic Church states "We must know Christ as the source of grace in order to know Adam as the source of sin." The pilgrim church of God "takes her place among the creatures which groan and travail yet await the revelation of the sons of God." (Romans 8:19-21) Thus this "truth of creation"—that the fundamental purpose of the lives of animals is not to serve the needs and desires of humans but to manifest God's glory—is affirmed through end-times theology. Humans share a common destiny of fellowship with God with other living creatures. Stated in Psalm 145:8-13, Revelation 5:4-13, Psalm 98:7-9, 1 Chronicles 16:30-34, both man and the creatures/creation praise the Lord together for all eternity.

Pope John Paul II states that man needs to respect "the nature of each being" within creation. He emphasizes that man has dominion over the animals but man does not have an absolute power. We do not have the right to "use and misuse," or to dispose of things for our own pleasures and convenience. Animals belong to God. He created them, therefore man has no right to alter them through genetic engineering. Each one of them is unique and wonderfully made and we have no right to interfere with what God has created. The animals exist primarily for God, not man, they belong to God. *For every beast of the forest is mine, and the cattle upon a thousand hills. I know all the fowls of the mountains: and the wild beasts of the field are mine.* (Psalm 50:10-11 KJV) The Pope said human patenting of animals is nothing less than idolatrous.

Based on Jewish and Christian tradition, and other religions as well, evidence from old manuscripts and Scriptures state that man will be held accountable before the almighty Lord for the way we have treated the animals here on earth. What a rude shock that will be for many Bible believers who have believed themselves exempt from the abuse, humane responsibility and neglect we have inflicted on His creation? And as to accountability for the animals Solomon summed it up when he said, "A righteous man has regard for his beast but the mercy of the wicked are cruel." (Proverbs 12:10 KJV)

Solomon's father David said, "The Lord is good to all, and his tender mercies are over all his works (His creation)...thou satisfiest the desire of every living thing." (Psalm 145:9 KJV) Though much of mankind lacks mercy for the creatures, God has mercy, eternal mercy for them.

What is the desire of every living, sentient being? As the word "instinct" means God-given intelligence, we know through scripture and simple observation that much of the non-human creatures have some intelligence. Certainly they are not to be tortured and die needlessly without any hope of a future state of righteousness.

How long shall the land mourn and the herbs of the whole field wither? For the wickedness of them that dwell therein, the beasts are consumed, and the birds; because they said: 'he seeth not our end.' They have made it a desolation, it mourneth unto Me, being desolate; the whole land is made desolate, because no man layeth it to heart. (Jeremiah 12:4, 11, Holy Scriptures)

Matthew Henry's commentary says of Jeremiah 12:4,11 God never did, and will never do anything wrong to any of His creatures. Matthew Henry goes on to say, "When we find it hard to understand particular providence we must have recourse to general truths as our first principles, and abide by them; however dark the province may be, the Lord is righteous."

To speak from the view of the animals and creation regarding Jeremiah 12:4, 11, as the animals are, in a true sense, speaking through the prophet Jeremiah as he views the world from the point of view of the creatures and creation as a whole. He says, "How long shall the land mourn and the herbs of the whole field wither? For the wickedness of man that dwells therein, we beasts are consumed and the birds; because man said: 'he seeth not our end' Man has made the world desolation. It mourneth unto God, because no man cares."

In the Open Bible, in Ecclesiastes, chapter 3, verses 16-22, the heading is "God judges righteous and wickedness." Solomon's father David, who wrote the Psalms, states that God judges the world with righteousness and the people with equity, His truth (equally). *Let the field be joyful, and all that is therein: then shall all the trees of the wood rejoice Before the Lord: for he cometh, for he cometh to judge the earth: he shall judge the world with righteousness, and the people with his truth.* (Psalm 96:12-13 KJV)

Let the sea roar, and the fullness thereof; the world, and they that dwell therein. Let the floods clap their hands: let the hills be joyful together before the LORD for he cometh to judge the earth: with righteousness shall he judge the world, and the people with equity (fairness). (Psalm 98:7-9, Open Bible)

In the Good News Bible under "The Goodness of God" we read: *LORD, your constant love reaches the heavens, your faithfulness extends to the skies. Your righteousness is towering like the mountains; your justice is like the depths of the sea. Men and animals are in your care.* (Psalms 36:5-6, Good News Bible)

A distinction is made between God's judgment and righteousness of the world/creation/earth and of the people. The world is judged with righteousness but the people are judged with equity/fairness. The word "with" means for, in correspondence, accompanying. It also can mean compared to. God compares the righteousness of creation with that of the people, the people being of a sinful nature, as compared to the creatures of an innocent nature.

Death came into the world only through the Devil's envy as those who belong to him find to their cost. (Wisdom 2:24 NJV) *But the souls of the upright are in the hands of God, and no torment can touch them.* (Wisdom 3:1 NJV)

But the upright live forever, their recompense is with the Lord, and the Most High takes care of them. (Wisdom 5:15 NJV) *For armour he will take his jealous love, he will arm creation to punish his enemies.* (Wisdom 5:17 NJV*) He will take up invincible holiness for shield, of his pitiless wrath he will forge a sword, and the universe will march with him to fight the reckless.* (Wisdom 5:20-21 NJV)

Your justice is as solid as God's mountains. Your decisions are as full of wisdom as the oceans are with water. You are concerned for men and animals alike. (Psalm 36:6 TLB)

Thy righteousness is like the great mountains; thy judgments are a great deep: O LORD, thou preservest man and beast. (Psalm 36:6, Criswell Study Bible) The Darby Bible says, "Thou savest man and beast." The Jewish Holy Scriptures says, *"Man and beast thou preservest, O LORD."*

As the 1700s concluded, a few theologians, philosophers, and even the science community maintained an understanding of the fact that the universe was not made just for man. This era, it seemed at least some extent, gave a kind of sympathy and felt a kinship between the species expanding our hearts to love and protect them. And as stated in *Love for Animals* by Dix Harwood in 1928, "If a man is entitled to immortality, then certainly beasts, which suffer all the consequences of man's depravity, will also be similarly rewarded. If living things are to have relations with one another, then we must settle as nearly as may be what the rights of each shall be in a world society. At any rate, we are all one, and the artificial inequalities must gradually disappear."

> He prayeth best, who loveth best
> All things both great and small;
> For the dear God who loveth us,
> He made and loveth all.

[Thus stated the true Christian by the end of the era; however, though they at that time had dreams that a new understanding of the ethical, humane treatment of animals would become legislation and abuse would cease, it for the most part did not stop. As the age of real materialism bloomed and man started searching the Bible for what promises were in it for himself, and himself alone, even more falsehood sprung up. People were told in Christian church after Christian church that animals did not go to heaven and had no soul or spirit, despite scriptures stating otherwise. Some in the ministry standing on John Calvin's one statement that animals were for our use only, failed to include Calvin's commentary and scriptural referencing that they do go to heaven. This presented man with the excuse to state animals did not deserve humane treatment, nor were they worthy of heaven. Those knowing the just God began to become suspect of some Christian churches and the ministry preaching untruths concerning the fair treatment and eternal life of animals. Instead of bringing people to salvation, some, through their false teachings have driven millions away from Jesus. — MBP]

Many of the popes of the Catholic faith, including Pope John Paul II, and the founders of the mainstream Protestant churches such as Martin Luther, John Calvin, and John Wesley, have writings and commentary quoting scripture to remind their congregations and future ones that animals do indeed go to heaven. In most cases they have also added commentary stating that all animals are to be treated humanely. Of all of the Christian faiths only the Vatican has in recent years written into their doctrine that animals are to be treated humanely and will be in heaven.

During the late 1700s many Christian theologians and moralists felt somewhat uncomfortable when they spoke of Genesis where man was given authority over everything that flies or creeps upon the earth. They realized that the animals did belong to God and that wanton destruction of them was an act of evil. Isaac Watts was a Calvinist; however, he disagreed with Calvin on the manner in which Calvin believed animals could be treated by mankind and had to question that of the evils beasts suffer in this world, there must be a better world hereafter for them. Before Eve sinned, all things were at peace. The evidence shows that man, once the favorite is now much nearer terms of equality with other living things, he said.

Reverend John Hildrop, MA, Rector of Wath, in Yorkshire, England, published a small book in 1742 in which he attacks the theory of a French Jesuit, Fr. Bourgeant. Fr. Bourgeant believed that the functions of brute creation were due to the evil spirits at work on earth. Rev. Hildrop also addresses the theory of the French philosopher and mathematician Descartes who in the early 1600s stated that animals were simply unfeeling machines.

Rev. Hildrop wrote, "In the beginning God appointed man the master of Eden; when he fell, his servants the animals went with him into outer darkness, even as in this life a man's family and retainers must suffer with the disgraced master. If death came into the world only after Adam's sin, then, before it came, animals must have been immortal. If they are intended for God's glory (and so is every created thing intended), then He will not slay them. When men assume that God will destroy, they conceive a wasteful deity; hence, an imperfect one. This God of ours made all things to be happy, yet animals have lost their primeval joy." And here the author rapped out a rebuke to the Bishop of Cork, Bishop Browne. The Bishop wanted no cheese mites in heaven. And the reply from Hildrop was "If God created the body of a cheese mite, will it be any more of a trick to endow it with a soul?"

Hildrop continued, "Genesis 9 authorized man to use beasts as food after the flood. Fear and dread now came upon all of the other species. What woe has our own kind wrought! The animals once roamed in peace, happy and innocent, wandering through the gardens and meadows of paradise. Yet after the flood the forests and land is filled with bloodshed and treachery. The very noblest fell the farthest. As in Eden the lion was the finest, so now he is the fiercest. The rest are now in a state of servitude to the very creatures who ruined them." Hildrop goes on to say, "They will be repaid one day for all they have suffered; they will be recompensed with life eternal; but in the meantime, common justice demands that they receive kindly treatment from those who brought damnation on them."

Rev. Hildrop wrote his account of Creation as written in the Book of Genesis. He asks: "Is there any thing in this account (the Book of Genesis) that seems either impossible or improbable? Does not the whole appear consistent, reasonable, worthy of God, and agreeable to Scriptures? On the other hand, how mean, how trifling, how unworthy of God, how repugnant to Scripture, is the philosophy of those, who suppose [animals] to be either animated by Evil Spirits or else allowing them no spiritual principle of motion or action, supposing them to be mere machines? Stating that they have no more sense or perception than a clock or a watch; that though they have some motion, some appearance of sense and shadow of reason, yet it is no more than what arises from the structure of their organs, and the mechanism of their frame; that they are therefore no more the objects of our compassion than any other piece of machinery...Is not this offering violence to reason, nature, and common sense? Is it not making a mockery of God's creatures?"

From the Holy Scriptures, Genesis 1:12, 18,21, 25, states "everything God made, He says was good." *And God made the beast of the earth after its kind, and the cattle after their kind, and every thing that creepeth upon the ground after its kind; and God saw that it was good.* (Genesis 1:25) In Genesis 1:22 God blessed all the creatures below man and said for them to multiply. In Genesis 1:27-29 God created man in His image. He blessed them and told them to multiply. God put man in dominion over the lower animals. ... *and to every fowl of the air, and to every thing that creepeth upon the earth, wherein there is a living soul, [I have given] every green herb for food.' And it was so. And God saw everything that He had made, and behold, it was very good. And there was evening and there was morning, the sixth day.*

Animals were blessed along with man. They were told to multiply and they were all created to go in pairs, male and female. They were given a soul as the original Jewish text reveals in Scripture. Then man sinned and brought physical death to all creation.

Rev. Hildrop says "[Adam] stood in the place of God to the world below him. He was the created image of the ever-blessed Trinity. Then by his transgression he lost the favor of his Maker, and forfeited both for us and the lower creation, the blessed privileges of our primitive state and condition; the communication of divine light and life between God and man. Now communication being suspended, he had no more power to direct and govern the creatures below him. He had no blessing to receive, and therefore none to bestow. The state of the brute creation, therefore, has, every since the fall of Man, been very different from what it was at the first."

[All were obedient to God's just commands until Eve and Adam ate of the tree of life in disobedience to God, being tricked by a creature the devil used to gain authority through man to become the prince of this world. — MBP]

Rev. Hildrop says: "Now I would venture to say, that the partition between the lowest degree of human and the highest degree of brute understanding, is so very slender, that it is hardly perceptible, and could not in any degree be distinguished but by a greater fluency of language; which, though in the main it may be considered an advantage to our species in general, yet is it none to those who seldom make any other use made of it, than to discover the emptiness of their heads, the perverseness of their wills, or the iniquity of their hearts, and show how little the real difference is (shape only excepted) between sagacious [having acute mental discernment and keen practical sense], good-natured, governable, useful animal, which we agree to call a brute; and a wrong-headed, vicious, ungovernable, mischievous brute, whom we agree to call a man; and what authority we have to strike out of the system of immortality so great a part of the creation without an absolute and evident necessity, exceeds my comprehension. If both reason and revelation assure, us, that in their first creation they were all very good: as perfect in their several kinds, as beautiful in their several orders, as necessary to the universal harmony, as infinite power and wisdom could make them; if by the special benediction of their Maker they were to increase and multiply, and perpetuate their several species, before sin and death entered into the world; how dare we pretend to reverse this blessing, to correct infinite wisdom, to alter the established order of things, and pronounce a sentence of utter extinction upon numerous ranks and orders of beings, created by infinite wisdom...

"Is not this pronouncing a curse where God has pronounced a blessing? And in effect declaring that Infinite Wisdom and power were idly employed in forming, supporting, feeding, and blessing numberless species, tribes and families of useless and unnecessary beings? Is it not more reasonable or consistent with the nature of God, and the scripture-account of the creation, to suppose that the immaterial forms, the incorruptible essence of the whole system, notwithstanding its present ruinous and deplorable appearance under the bondage of corruption and death, are immoveably fixed in their proper rank and order in the invisible world, according to the eternal archetypal model (original form) in the divine mind, in and by which, as their efficient and exemplary cause, every being in heaven and earth, from the most exalted seraph to the lowest vegetable, was made, in which they now subsist, and shall for ever subsist, in a glorious immortality?"

How lovely is your Temple, O Lord of the armies of heaven. I long, yes, faint with longing to be able to enter your courtyard and come near to the Living God. Even the sparrows and swallows are welcome to come and nest among your altars and there have their young, O Lord of heaven's armies, my King and my God! How happy are those who can live in your Temple, singing your praises. (Psalm 84:1-4 Good News Bible)

Deuteronomy 5:14, Exodus 19:10 and Exodus 23:12 say the animals were to rest along with man on the seventh day. *Six days thou shalt do thy work, but on the seventh day thou shalt rest: that thine ox and thine ass may rest...* (Exodus 23:12, Holy Scriptures)

Rev. Dr. T. Dewitt Talmage was a noted Presbyterian minister in Brooklyn, New York City. He was born in 1832 and died in 1902. Within his very popular and vast collection of sermons he speaks on the subject of animals: "Behold in the first place, that on the first night of Christ's life God honored the animal creation. You cannot get into that Bethlehem barn without going past the camels, the mules, the dogs, and the oxen. The animals of that stable heard the first cry of the infant Lord. Some of the old painters represent the oxen and camels kneeling that night before the new-born babe. And well might they kneel. Have you ever thought that Christ came, among other things, to alleviate the sufferings of the animal creation? Was it not appropriate that He should, during the first few days and nights of His life on earth, be surrounded by the dumb beasts whose moans and plaint have for ages been a prayer to God for the arresting of their tortures and the righting of their wrongs? It did not merely 'happen so,' that the unintelligent creatures of God should have been that night in close neighborhood. Not a kennel in all the centuries, not a robbed bird's nest, not a worn-out horse on the towpath, not a herd freezing in the poorly-built cow-pen, not a freight car bringing the beeves to market without water through a thousand miles of agony, not a surgeon's room witnessing the struggles of the fox or rabbit or pigeon or dog in the horrors of vivisection, but has an interest in the fact that Christ was born in a stable surrounded by animals. He remembers that night, and the prayer He heard in their pitiful moan. He will answer in the punishment of those who maltreat them."

CHAPTER 5

Dr. Albert Schweitzer and His Reverence for Life

References:

- ✒ Ann Cottrell Free, editor, *Animals, Nature and Albert Schweitzer*
- ✒ Albert Schweitzer, *The Philosophy of Civilization*

*D*r. Albert Schweitzer was a famous medical doctor whose humble spirit and love for all creation led him to Africa to treat the poorest of humanity who had not financial means to acquire medical attention.

"As long as I can remember, I have suffered because of the great misery I saw in the world. I never really knew the youthful joy of living. I believe that many children feel this way," Dr. Albert Schweitzer stated concerning his childhood.

Before he entered primary school he composed a small prayer: "Dear God, protect and bless all living things. Keep them from evil and let them sleep in peace."

"I suffered particularly because the poor animals must endure so much pain and want," Schweitzer explained. "The sight of an old, limping horse being dragged along by one man while another man struck him with a stick—he was being driven to the Colmar slaughterhouse—haunted me for weeks."

Schweitzer says of Nature: "The deeper we look into nature, the more we realize that it is full of life and the more profoundly we know that all life is sacred and that we are united with all life that is in nature. Man can no longer live for himself alone. We must realize that all life is valuable and that we are united to all life. From this knowledge comes our spiritual relationship to the universe.

The fact that in nature one creature may cause pain to another, and even deal with it instinctively in the most cruel way, is a harsh mystery that weighs upon us as long as we live. One who has reached the point where he does not suffer ever again because of this has ceased to be a man."

Dr. Schweitzer says, "Whenever an animal is somehow forced into the service of men, every one of us must be concerned for any suffering it bears on that account. No one may shut his eyes and think the pain, which is therefore not visible to him, is non-existent.

"Each of us must therefore decide whether to condemn living creatures to suffering and death out of inescapable necessity, and thus incur guilt. The man who pledges himself to neglect no opportunity to help creatures in distress can find some atonement for guilt."

These are the things Dr. Schweitzer accepts as being Good: "To preserve life, to promote life, to raise to its highest value life which is capable of development"; and, as being Evil: "To destroy life, to repress life which is capable of development. This is the absolute, fundamental principle of the moral, and it is the necessity of thought."

Dr. Schweitzer asks when will we reach a time when hunting, the pleasure of killing animals for sport, will be regarded as a mental aberration? "We must reach the point when killing for sport will be felt as a disgrace to our civilization."

He truly loved and appreciated God's creatures and understood their intelligence, feelings, love and fears and he so loved being around the animals all the time.

In *The Philosophy of Civilization* Dr. Schweitzer says the moral for which man should attain is of concern for all creation. He says, "If one walks on the road after a shower and sees an earthworm which has strayed on to it, he bethinks himself that it must get dried up in the sun if it does not return soon enough to ground into which it can burrow, so he lifts it from the deadly stone surface and puts it on the grass. He should not be afraid of being laughed at for such a sentimental act. It is the fate of every truth to be laughed at until it is recognized."

He speaks of the reverence for life concerning the relationship between man and the animal world: "Whenever one injures an animal of any kind one must consider if it is truly necessary." He speaks of inoculating animals with diseases, and so as to be able to bring help to mankind with the results gained. "These people must never quiet any misgivings they feel with the general reflection that their cruel proceedings aim at a valuable result. They must first have considered in each individual case whether there is a real necessity to force upon any animal this sacrifice for the sake of mankind. And they must take the most anxious care to mitigate as much as possible the pain inflicted. He reminds us that everyone must be concerned with what the suffering every animal does for the benefit of mankind.

"No one must shut his eyes and regard as non-existent the sufferings of which he spares himself the sight. Let no one regard as light the burden of his responsibility. While so much ill-treatment of animals goes on, while the moans of thirsty animals in railway trucks sound unheard, while so much brutality prevails in our slaughter-houses, while animals have to suffer in our kitchens painful death from unskilled hands, while animals have to endure intolerable treatment from heartless men, or are left to the cruel play of children, we all share the guilt.

"The ethics of reverence for life guards us from letting each other believe through our silence that we no longer experience what, as thinking men, we must experience. They make us join in keeping on the look-out for opportunities of bringing some sort of help to animals, to make up for the great misery which men inflict on them, and thus to step for a moment out of the incomprehensible horror of existence."

The Life of Dr. Albert Schweitzer

Albert Schweitzer lived from 1875 though 1965, the son of a Lutheran minister. He grew up in an Alastian village. He studied organ in Paris and was in the military service. He became a professional organist and published his first book before 1899. Schweitzer received a doctorate of philosophy at the University of Strasbourg in 1899. He received a degree in theology and was ordained as a pastor in 1900. He continued his professional career as an organist, a pastor of a church and was the principal of a theological seminary.

This, however, was not what he felt God wanted for his life, and in 1905 at the age of thirty he felt led to study medicine and go to Africa to help those who were too poor to afford medical treatment. In 1912 he married Helene Bresslau, and in 1913 after finishing his M.D., the couple left for Africa to set up a hospital to treat the poor.

In 1917 the French forced the Schweitzers to go to France as civilian interns until the end of the war. In 1919 their daughter Rhena was born and five years later he returned to Africa alone to rebuild his hospital in a new location. He continued to travel, giving lectures and concerts. Mrs. Schweitzer joined him, escaping from Europe during the Second World War.

In 1952 he received the Nobel Peace Prize and Medal from the Animal Welfare Institute. In 1957, his wife, Helene, died in Switzerland. Dr. Schweitzer continued his fight for the rights of animals and endorsed a bill in the U.S. Senate to reduce laboratory animal suffering. In March 1965, the government of Africa, due to the fear of the spread of rabies, ordered all of his dogs, cats, and monkeys be put to death. His love for animals was so great and his lifetime of suffering over the pain inflicted on animals took such an emotional toll that he passed away within seven months of their deaths at the age of 90.

His most famous book, *The Philosophy of Civilization,* in which he wrote his great discourse "Reverence for Life," has helped mold modern thought toward more compassion for the non-human creation and that of mankind as well. In his lifetime he never missed an opportunity to demonstrate his compassion for both man and animals. His teachings and examples affected people all over the world as he became recognized as a leading advocate for the welfare of the animal kingdom and fight to save man from himself in teaching the value of all life on earth and the preservation of all that God has created as much as possible.

He prayed continuously for the protection of the animals and for the minds of man to be opened to the understanding of concern for creation. He wrote that he could never be at complete peace even through all of his honors and accomplishments because he was constantly in remembrance of the suffering of humanity and the animals. He knew so much of creation was suffering needlessly at the hands of mankind, bringing excruciating pain in the name of science or sport.

CHAPTER 6

Obedience of Creation and
The Faithfulness of God

References:
- Matthew Henry, *Commentary*

*W*hen considering the obedience of the animals, the Bible reveals many were obedient to God, and Psalm 119:89-96 addresses all of God's servants. His servants are the angels, the saints, and the non-human animals as well. *For ever, O Lord, Thy word standeth fast in heaven. Thy faithfulness is unto all generations; Thou hast established the earth, and it standeth. They stand this day according to Thine ordinances; for all things are Thy servants. Unless Thy law had been my delight, I should then have perished in mine affliction.* (Psalm 119:89-92 Holy Scriptures)

Matthew Henry's commentary on Psalm 119:89-91 states, "Your faithfulness continues through all generations. He produces, for proof of it, the constancy of the course of nature: You established the earth, and it endures. It is by virtue of God's promise to Noah (Gen. 8:22) that day and night, summer and winter, observe a steady course. All the creatures are, in their places, and according to their capacities, useful to their Creator, and fulfill the purpose of their creation; and shall man be the only rebel, the only revolter from his allegiance, and the only unprofitable burden of the earth?"

A prophet named Elijah, from Tishbe in Gilead, said to King Ahab, "In the name of the LORD, the living God of Israel, whom I serve, I tell you that there will be no dew or rain for the next two or three years until

I say so." Then the LORD said to Elijah, *"Leave this place and go west and hide yourself near Cherith Brook, east of the Jordan. The brook will supply you with water to drink, and I have commanded ravens to bring you food there."* Elijah obeyed the Lord's command, and went and stayed by Cherith Brook. He drank water from the brook, and ravens brought him bread and meat every morning and every evening.* (1 Kings 17:1-6 Good News Bible) This is an example of animals doing the will of God as He commanded them to bring food to Elijah.

1 Kings 13:18-29 tells of a prophet from Judah who disobeyed God, as God had told him not to eat or drink anything which King Jeroboam or anyone else offered him and to return home a different way than he had come; but when the prophet in Bethel tempted him, he disobeyed God and was killed by a lion. This is an example in line with the whale that swallowed Jonah and the donkey of Balaam of an animal being obedient to the Lord. *Then the old prophet from Bethel said to him, "I, too, am a prophet just like you, and at the Lord's command an angel told me to take you home with me and offer you my hospitality." But the old prophet was lying. So the prophet from Judah went home with the old prophet and had a meal with him. As they were sitting at the table, the word of the LORD came to the old prophet, and he cried out to the prophet from Judah, "The LORD says that you disobeyed him and did not do what he commanded. Instead, you returned and ate a meal in a place he had ordered you not to eat in. Because of this you will be killed, and your body will not be buried in your family grave." After they had finished eating, the old prophet saddled the donkey for the prophet from Judah, who rode off. On the way a lion met him and killed him. His body lay on the road, and the donkey and the lion stood beside it. Some men passed by and saw the body on the road, with the lion standing near by. They went on into Bethel and reported what they had seen. When the old prophet heard about it, he said, "That is the prophet who disobeyed the Lord's command! And so the LORD sent the lion to attack and kill him, just as the LORD said he would." Then he said to his sons, "Saddle my donkey for me." They did so, and he rode off and found*

the prophet's body lying on the road, with the donkey and the lion still standing by it. The lion had not eaten the body or attacked the donkey. The old prophet picked up the body, put it on the donkey, and brought it back to Bethel to mourn over it and bury it. (1 Kings 13:18-29 Good News Bible)

Exodus 19:12-13 tells us that neither man nor beast could touch the mountain where Moses went to get the Ten Commandments or they would die. *There shall not an hand touch it, but he shall surely be stoned, or shot through; whether it be beast or man, it shall not live: when the trumpet soundeth long, they shall come up to the mount.* (Exodus 19:13 KJV)

Balaam was a very disobedient prophet. He did not want to do as the Lord commanded him to not curse the people of Israel as the King of Moab, Balak, so wanted. However, Balaam went with the prince of Moab to curse the Israelites, which made the Lord very angry so God sent an angel to stop him. Balaam had his ass and his two servants with him. *And the ass saw the angel of the LORD standing in the way, and his sword drawn in his hand: and the ass turned aside out of the way, and went into the field: and Balaam smote the ass, to turn her into the way. But the angel of the LORD stood in a path of the vineyards, a wall being on this side, and a wall on that side. And when the ass saw the angel of the LORD, she thrust herself unto the wall, and crushed Balaam's foot against the wall: and he smote her again. And the angel of the LORD went further, and stood in a narrow place, were was no way to turn either to the right hand or to the left. And when the ass saw the angel of the LORD, she fell down under Balaam: and Balaam's anger was kindled, and he smote the ass with a staff. And the LORD opened the mouth of the ass, and she said unto Balaam, What have I done unto thee, that thou hast smitten me these three times? And Balaam said unto the ass, Because thou hast mocked me: I would there were a sword in mine hand, for now would I kill thee. And the ass said unto Balaam, Am not I thine ass, upon which thou has ridden ever since I was thine unto this day? Was I ever wont to do so unto thee? And he said, Nay. Then the LORD opened the eyes of Balaam, and he saw the*

*angel of the LORD standing in the way, and his sword drawn in his hand:
and he bowed down his head, and fell flat on his face. And the angel of the
Lord said unto him, Wherefore has thou smitten thine ass these three times?
Behold, I went out to withstand thee, because thy was in perverse before me;
and the ass saw me, and turned from me these three times; unless she had
turned from me, surely now also I had slain thee, and saved her alive.*
(Numbers 22:23-33 KJV)

There is so much unnatural to human understanding in this message. We have a disobedient man and an obedient donkey. We have a
donkey that can see an angel (a spirit being), and we have a donkey
that can also talk as commanded by God. And we have a man who has
no problem believing that the donkey can talk and talks back. If we
outside of the Bible tried to convince someone of this type of situation
it would be most improbable if not impossible.

*Now the Lord had prepared a large fish to swallow up Jonah. And
Jonah was in the belly of the fish three days and three night. Now Jonah
prayed to the Lord for deliverance. And the LORD spake unto the fish, and
it vomited out Jonah upon the dry land.* (Jonah 1:17 and 2:10 KJV)

In the Book of Jonah, chapters 1-4, the prophet was no better in
obeying the Lord than Balaam was. And as a result he was swallowed
by a very large fish and lived to tell about it. Jonah was told by God to
go to Nineveh and tell them of their wickedness but he got on a boat
and headed the other direction. The Lord caused great turbulence in
the water and those aboard decided to cast lots, as surely one on board
was evil and the one on whom the lot fell would be cast out of the
boat. The lot fell on Jonah and he confessed his sin so there was no
question as to who was going overboard. As he was thrown out of the
boat the Lord had a very large fish waiting for him, and with one big
gulp Jonah found himself in the belly of the whale. He remained there
three days and then the Lord told the fish to belch Jonah upon dry
land. The fish followed the command of the Lord and both man and
fish lived on. But the Lord had gotten Jonah's attention by now and
did go to the City of Nineveh and tell this sinful people to repent.

Jonah begrudgingly went to them telling them to fast; both man and beast were to refrain from eating any food or drinking any water. Both man and beast had to be covered with sackcloth and cry mightily unto God and repent.

CHAPTER 7

All Creation Praise the Lord Forever

*I*n the Book of Daniel there are numerous verses which have been removed from the Protestant Bible. They refer to all creation praising God. The verses go between Daniel 3:23 and 3:24 and are referred to as *The Prayer of Azahiah and the Song of the Three Jews.* The Book of Daniel is about three men, Shadrach, Meshach, and Abednego. Nebuchadnezzar the ruler of Babylon who besieged Jerusalem and overtook it required everyone to worship and obey the rules of the land set down by King Nebuchadnezzar and when they would not bow down to him they were thrown into a fiery furnace, from which God delivered them. Within the verses there are numerous mentions by the three of them stating that all creation is to praise God forever. nd though much of this has been removed from the Protestant Bible it is very important that we understand the significance of creation and their praising to God. I am using the earliest text I could find, and due to the translations, the names of the three men mentioned in the 1609 version of the Douay Rehims Bible is different from the Protestant version. The three names appear as Ananias, Azarias, and Misael until after they come out of the furnace when King Nabuchodonosor (Nebuchadnezzar in KJV Protestant Bible) refer to them as Sidrach, Misach, and Abednego in the Douay Rheims Catholic version.

(46) Now The King's servants that had cast them in, ceased not to heat of the furnace with brimstone, and tow, and pitch, and dry sticks, (47) And the flame mounted up above the furnace nine and forty cubits: (48) And it broke forth, and burnt such of the Chaldeans as it found near the furnace, (49) But the angel of the Lord went into the furnace:

and he drove the flames of the fire out of the furnace, (50) And made the midst of the furnace like the blowing of a wind bringing dew, and the fire touched them not at all, nor troubled them, nor did them any harm. (51) Then these three as with one mouth praised, and glorified, and blessed God in the furnace, saying (52) "Blessed are thou, O Lord, the God of our fathers: and worthy to be praised and glorified, and exalted above all for ever: and blessed is the holy name of thy glory: and worthy to be praised, and exalted above all in all ages. (56) Blessed are thou in the firmament of heaven: and worthy of praise and glorious for ever. (57) All ye works of the Lord, bless the Lord: praise and exalt him above all for ever. (59) O ye angels of the Lord bless the Lord: praise and exalt him above all for ever." (Daniel 3: 46-59 Douay Rheims Version)

Verses 59-64 speak of the heavens, waters, sun, moon, stars, dew, all the elements God has created are to praise God. We find similar verses of praise to God by all creation in the Book of Psalms.

(65) O all ye spirits of God, bless the Lord: praise and exalt him above all for ever. (74) O let the earth bless the Lord: let it praise and exalt him above all for ever. (75) O ye mountains and hills, bless the Lord: praise and exalt him above all for ever. (76) O all ye things that springs up in the earth, bless the Lord: praise and exalt him above all for ever. (77) O ye fountains, bless the Lord: praise and exalt him above all for ever. (78) O ye seas and rivers, bless the Lord: praise and exalt him above all for ever. (79) O ye whales, and all that move in the waters, bless the Lord: praise and exalt him above all for ever. (80) O all ye fowls of the air, bless the Lord: praise and exalt him above all for ever. (81) O all ye beasts and cattle, bless the Lord: praise and exalt him above all for ever. (82) O ye sons of men, bless the Lord: praise and exalt him above all for ever. (83) O let Israel bless the Lord: let them praise and exalt him above all for ever. (84) O ye priests of the Lord, bless the Lord: praise and exalt him above all for ever. (85) O ye servants of the Lord, bless the Lord: praise and exalt him above all for ever. (86) O ye spirits and souls of the just, bless the Lord: praise and exalt him above all for ever. (87) O ye holy and humble of heart, bless the Lord: praise and exalt him above all for

ever. (88) O Ananias, Azarias, and Misael, bless ye the Lord: praise and exalt him above all for ever. For he hath delivered us from hell, and saved us out of the hand of death, and delivered us out of the midst of the burning flame, and saves us out of the midst of the fire. (89) O give thanks to the Lord because he is good: because his mercy endureth for ever and ever. (91 Then Nabuchodonosor the king was astonished, and rose up in haste, and said to his nobles: did we not cast three men bound into the midst of the fire? They answered the king, and said: True, O king. (92) He answered and said: Behold I see four men loose, and walking in the midst of the fire, and there is no hurt in them, and the form of the fourth is like the Son of God. (93) Then Nabuchodonosor came to the door of the burning fiery furnace, and said: Sidrach, Misach, and Abdenago, ye servants of the most high God, go ye forth, and come. And immediately Sidrach, Misach, and Abdenago went out from the midst of the fire. (Daniel 3:65-93 Douay Rheims Version)

[An interesting side note: The King noticed the fourth figure in the furnace and to him that figure was like the Son of God. We are in the Old Testament yet this is a reference to Jesus the Messiah who has not yet physically come to earth. — MBP]

King David praised God continually. In the Book of Psalms he speaks of all creation praising God. Within both the Books of Daniel and Psalms the writers continuously include all creation. *(1) Praise ye the Lord. Praise ye the Lord from the heavens: praise him in the heights. (2) Praise ye him, all his angels: praise ye him, all his host. (3) Praise ye him, sun and moon: praise him, all ye stars of light. (4) Praise him, ye heavens of heavens, and ye waters that be above the heavens. (5) Let them praise the name of the Lord: for he commanded and they were created. (6) He hath also stablished them for ever and ever: he hath made a decree, which shall not pass. (7) Praise the Lord from the earth, ye dragons, and all deeps: (8) Fire, and hail; snow, and vapours; stormy wind fulfilling his word: (9) Mountains, and all hills: fruitful trees, and all cedars; (10) Beasts, and all cattle; creeping things, and flying fowl: (11) Kings of the earth, and all people; princes, and all judges of the earth: (12) both young men, and maidens; old men and children: (13) Let them praise the name of the Lord; for his name alone is excellent; his glory is above the earth and heaven. (14) He also exalteth the horn of his people, and praise of all his saints; even for the children of Israel, a people near unto him. Praise ye the Lord.* (Psalm 148:1-14 KJV)

Hail, snow and clouds, strong winds that obey his command. Praise him, hills and mountains, fruit trees and forests; all animals, tame and wild, reptiles and birds. Praise him, kings and all peoples, princes and all other rulers; girls and young men old people and children too. Let them all praise the name of the LORD! His name is greater than all others; his glory is above earth and heaven. (Psalm 148:7-13 Good News Bible)

In Psalm 104 David speaks of God creating everything and he then adds how God takes the breath (spirit) of all the living back to Himself, and then He sends His spirit and new life in formed on the earth to replace the lost. *(19) He assigned the moon to mark the months, and the sun to make the days. (20) He sends the night and darkness, when all the forest folk come out. (21) Then the young lions roar for their food, but they are dependent on the Lord. (22) At dawn they slink back into their dens to rest, (23) and men go off to work until the evening shadows fall again. (24) O Lord, what a variety you have made! And in wisdom you have made them all! The earth is full of your riches. (25) There before me lies the mighty ocean teeming with life of every kind, both great and small. (26) And look! See the ships! And over there, the whale you made to play in the sea. (27) Every one of these depends on you to give them daily food. (28) You supply it, and they gather it. You open wide your hand to feed them and they are satisfied with all your bountiful provision. (29) But if you turn away from them, then all is lost. And when you gather up their breath, they die and return again to dust. (30) Then you send your Spirit, and new life is born to replenish all the living of the earth. (31) Praise God forever! How he must rejoice in all his work!* (Psalm 104:19-31 TLB)

And every creature which is in heaven, and on the earth and under the earth, and such as are in the sea, and all that are in them, heard I saying, Blessing, and honour, and glory, and power, be unto him that sitteth upon the throne, and unto the Lamb for ever and ever. (Revelations 5:13 KJV)

Bless ye the LORD, all ye his hosts; ye ministers of his that do his pleasure Bless the LORD, all his works in all places of his dominion: bless the LORD, O my soul. (Psalm 103:21-22, Open Bible)

I will always praise the Lord; let all his creatures praise his holy name forever. (Psalm 145:21 Good News Bible)

Praise the LORD from the earth, sea monsters and all ocean depths. (Psalm 148:7 NAB) *Let everything that hath breath praise the LORD. Praise ye the LORD.* (Psalm 150:6 KJV)

Let everything everywhere bless the Lord. And now I bless him too! (Psalm 103:22 TLB)

All your creatures, LORD, will praise you, and all your people will give you thanks. They will speak of the glory of your royal power and tell of your might, so that everyone will know your mighty deeds and the glorious majesty of your kingdom. Your rule is eternal, and you are king forever. The Lord is faithful to his promises, and everything he does is good. He helps those who are in trouble; he lifts those who have fallen. All living things look hopefully to you, and you give them food when they need it. You give them enough and satisfy the needs of all. The LORD is righteous in all he does, merciful in all his acts. He is near to those who call to him, who call to him with sincerity. He supplies the needs of those who honor him; he hears their cries and saves them. He protects everyone who loves him, but he will destroy the wicked. (Psalm 145:10-20 Good News Bible)

The many and various versions of scriptures revealing the praising to God by all creation should give one an understanding of the importance of praising God and open our minds to the possibility that the non-human creation must in ways we do not understand praise God and see beyond this world. It is sin which makes man blind to the real understanding and wisdom of God. Sin is not found among the remainder of creation below man, thus they are not subject to the spiritual blindness, which has separated us from much of the truths of God.

[In closing this chapter I want to add the importance of praising God in all things—*all* things. Many people call or e-mail me hurting so much from losing their beloved pet. The Bible says to praise God in all things, and as hard as it may seem, that is what I do when I have lost a loved one or a beloved pet. I cry and I hurt deeply but I have found that the assurance of their eternal existence and presence now in heaven gives me comfort and peace even through the tears and then I have to discipline myself to say, "Mary, your work on earth is not finished and this is part of what God already knew you would be going through. It is time now to go on with your mission in this life and make a better earthly stay for others both human and non-human creation so just keep on keeping on." — MBP]

CHAPTER 8

Pope John Paul II and The Roman Catholic Church

References:

- ❧ Pope John Paul II, *Crossing the Threshold of Hope*
- ❧ Pope John Paul II, *God, Father, and Creator*
- ❧ First Vatican Council *Constitution Dei Filius*
- ❧ Pope John Paul II, *Quotable John Paul II*
- ❧ Pope John Paul II, *In My Own Words*

In *Crossing the Threshold of Hope,* Pope John Paul II states that man is saved by grace in Christ alone and that "no man cometh to the father except through the son. For there is one God. There is also one mediator between God and the human race, Christ Jesus, himself human (1 Timothy 2:5). There is no salvation through any other name (Acts 4:12). It is therefore a revealed truth that there is salvation only and exclusively in Christ."

Pope John Paul II has also addressed the vain attitude and neglect of mankind concerning the non-human world bringing to light the love the Creator has for them, not only now but for all eternity.

Pope John Paul II says of the Gospel: "The Gospel means 'good news.' God, who is creating, saw that His creation was good, it was very good (Genesis 1:1-25). The Gospel is the source of joy for all creatures, and above all for humankind. His joy spreads especially through the 'good news,' according to which good is greater than all which is evil in the world. Creation was given and entrusted to humankind as a duty, representing not a source of suffering but the foundation of a creative existence in the world."

The Pope says of mankind's responsibility of creation: "A person who believes in the essential goodness of all creation is capable of discovering all the secrets of creation in order to perfect continually the work assigned to him by God."

The Second Vatican Council, rooted in the Mystery of the Trinity, says: "At the heart of the Church is Christ and His Sacrifice, a Sacrifice celebrated in a certain sense on the altar of all creation, on the altar of the world. Christ 'is the firstborn of all creation.' (Colossians1:15) Through His Resurrection He is also 'the firstborn from the dead.' (Col.1:18) Around His redemptive sacrifice is gathered all creation, which is working out its eternal destiny in God. If this process causes pain, it is, however, full of hope, as Saint Paul teaches in the Letter to the Romans (Romans 8:23-24)."

Salvation not only confronts evil in each of its existing forms in this world, it proclaims victory over evil. Moreover, the Pope states: "The work of redemption of man elevates creation to a new level. Christ swallowed up death through his resurrection."

[Hope means assurance. It is the assurance of things not seen, yet to come. — MBP]

In *God, Father, and Creator,* Pope John Paul II says, "For by the very circumstance of their having been created, all things are endowed with their own stability, truth, goodness, proper laws, and order. Man must respect these as he isolates them by the appropriate methods of the individual sciences or arts.

God, who through the Word creates all things (John 1:3) and keeps them in existence, gives men an enduring witness to himself in created realities (Romans 1:19-20).

Pope John Paul II addresses the true Gospel of Life, *Evangelism Vitae,* which speaks of the goodness of all creatures and reminds us that according to the Bible the animals belong not to man but to God Himself, their Creator. All creatures are created to celebrate God in a manner appropriate to the form of life they have been designated by God. *He has made everything beautiful in its time... I know that whatever God does endures forever; nothing can be added to it, nor anything taken from it.* (Ecclesiastes 3:11,14)

The Pope quotes the Book of Wisdom to further reveal the praises of God for the love with which he created the universe and keeps it in existence: *For you love all things that exist, and loathe nothing of the things which you have made, for you would not have made anything if you had hated it. How would anything have endured if you had not willed it? Or how would anything not called forth by you have been preserved? You spare all things, for they are yours, O Lord who loves the living.* (Wisdom 11:24-26)

The Pope speaks of the importance of God's will, his love, and his omnipotence. "The Creator's omnipotence is shown both in calling creatures into existence from nothingness and also in maintaining them in existence. As quoted in the Book of Wisdom 11:24-26, His omnipotence shows His love who, in creation gives existence to beings different from himself, and at the same time different among themselves. The reality of his gift permeates the whole being and existence of creation. To create means to give, and especially to give existence. And he who gives, loves. God loves all things that exist, and loathes none of the things, which he has made, and He spares all things, for they belong to Him, the Lord who loves all the living."

Pope John Paul II states: "God the Creator is He 'who accomplishes all things according to the counsel of his will' (Ephesians 1:11). The whole work of creation belongs to the plan of salvation, 'the mystery hidden for ages in God who created all things' (Ephesians 3:9). Through the act of the creation of the world, and especially of man, the plan of salvation begins to be realized as mentioned in many scriptures including Proverbs 8:22-35."

"It is clear that the truth of faith about creation is radically opposed to the theories of materialistic philosophy. These view the cosmos as the result of an evolution of matter reducible to pure chance and necessity," explains the Pope.

"It is a truth of faith that the world has its beginning in the creator, who is the Triune God. Although the work of creation is attributed especially to God the Father—this we profess in the creeds of the faith ("I believe in God the Father Almighty, Creator of heaven and earth")—it is also a truth of faith that the Father, the Son and the Holy Spirit are the unique and indivisible 'principle' of creation.

"In the Old Testament such as Psalm 33:6 and in the New Testament John says *'In the beginning was the Word, and the Word was God...all things were made through him, and without him nothing was made...and the world was made through him* (John 1:1-2,10). In 1 Corinthians 8:6 Paul says everything was made 'in Jesus Christ.' St. Paul speaks of 'one Lord, Jesus Christ, through whom are all things and through whom we exist.' *He (Christ) is the image of the invisible God, the first-born of all creation; for in him all things were created, in heaven and on earth, visible and invisible...all things were created through him and for him. He is before all things, and in him all thing hold together.* (Colossians 1:15-17).

"The active presence of Christ is described both as the cause of creation ('through him') and as its final cause ('for him'). Hebrews states God through the Son 'also created the world' and that the "Son...upholds the universe by his word of power."

"Especially St. Paul and St. John in the New Testament deepens and enriches the creative Word already present in the Old Testament: *By the word of the Lord the heavens were made.* (Psalm 33:6). It makes clear that the creative Word was not 'with God,' only but it *'was* God.' The Son consubstantial (coexisting, having like nature) with the Father, the Word created the world in union with the Father. *And the world was made through him.* (John 1: 1,2,10) Colossians 1:15 reveals the Word, who is the Eternal Son reflecting the glory of God and bearing the very stamp of his nature. Hebrews 1:3 says 'he who is the first born of all creation' and in the sense that all things have been created in the Word-Son, to become, in time, the word of God. In this sense "all things were made through him, and without him nothing was made." (John 1:3).

"Creation, then, is the work of the Triune God. The world "created" in the Word-Son, is "restored" together with the Son to the Father, through that Uncreated Gift, the Holy Spirit, coexisting with both. In this way the world is created in that Love, which is the Spirit of the Father and of the Son. This universe embraced by eternal Love begins to exist in the instant chosen by the Trinity at the beginning of time."

[Creation of the world is the work of love, unending, unceasing, eternal love. — MBP]

Pope John Paul II continues: "The new dimension of God's glory begins with the creation of the visible and invisible world." He cites the following scriptures: *The heavens declare the glory of God; and the firmament proclaims his handiwork... There is no speech, nor are there words whose sound is not heard. Their voice goes out through all the earth, and their words to the end of the world.* (Psalms 19:1,2,4) *The sun looks down on everything with its light and the work of the Lord is full of his glory.* (Sirach 42:16) *The stars shone in their watches and were glad; he called them, and they said, 'Here we are!' They shone with gladness for him who made them.* (Baruch 3:34) *O all you works of the Lord, bless the Lord, to him be highest glory and praise forever.* (Daniel 3:57) *Make a joyful noise to God, all the earth; sing the glory of his name: give to him glorious praise! Say to God, 'How glorious are your deeds! So great is your power that your enemies cringe before you. All the earth worships you; they sing praises to you, sing praises to your name.'* (Psalms 66:1-4) *O Lord, how manifold are your works! In wisdom you have made them all, the earth is full of your creatures.* (Psalm 104:24) *All the earth shall be filled with the glory of the Lord.* (Numbers 14:21).

The First Vatican Council addresses the concern for creation, both man and beast, and about the Creator who brought it all into being. It states: "This one true God in his goodness and omnipotent power, not to increase his own happiness nor to acquire, but to manifest his perfection through the gifts he distributes to creatures, by a supremely free decision, simultaneously from the beginning of time drew forth from nothingness both the one creature and the other, the spiritual and the corporeal..."

Wisdom and love of God, the Pope says, are the principal and end of creation. The mystery of God's glory is realized in creation. *O all you works of the Lord, bless the Lord.* (Daniel 3:57) All creatures receive their superior meaning in the mystery of that glory.

O Lord, how manifold are your works! In wisdom you have made them all; the earth is full of your creatures. May the glory of the Lord endure forever, may the Lord rejoice in his works. I will sing to the Lord as long as I live; I will sing to my God all my life. (Psalm 104:24,31,33)

The First Vatican Council's *Constitution Dei Filius* expresses God's absolute liberty in creation and his every action. God is "most happy in himself and of himself." He possesses the complete fullness of goodness and happiness in himself and of himself. He does not call the world into existence in order to complete or integrate the goodness, which he is. But he did call the creatures into existence by a totally free and sovereign decision. And in a limited and partial way, they do participate in the perfection of God's absolute fullness. Though they have differing degrees of perfection from the inanimate, animate and to a higher degree to human beings.

He creates solely and exclusively for the purpose of bestowing the goodness of a manifold existence on the world of invisible and visible creatures. It is a multiple and varied participation of the unique, infinite, eternal good, which is identical with the very Being of God. *I am the Lord, who made all things, who stretched out the heavens alone, who spread out the earth—who was with me?* (Isaiah 44:24)

Pope John Paul II explains love: "Love means precisely this¯to will the good, to adhere to the good. From this eternal will of the Good there gushes from the infinite goodness of God in regard to creatures and, in particular, in regard to man. Love is the origin of God's clemency, of his readiness to give freely and to pardon. Love is expressed in providence by which God continues and sustains the world of creation. Through redemption and justification, it guides man to his own sanctification by the power of the Holy Spirit.

It concerns God who, as a wise and omnipotent Father, is present and active in the world and in the history of every creature. He does this so that every creature, and specifically man, God's image, may be able to live life as a journey under the guidance of truth and love toward the goal of eternal life in God.

God continues to declare himself, as in the first moment of creation, in favor of being as opposed to nothing, in favor of life as opposed to death, in favor of "light" as opposed to "darkness." (John 1:4-5) "God saw that it was good...that it was very good." (Genesis 1:25, 31) That constitutes the fundamental and unshakable affirmation of the work of creation.

First Vatican Council states that "All that God created, he conserves and directs by his Providence" reaching from end to end mightily and governing all things well." (Wisdom 8:1) "All that God has created, he watches over and governs by his divine Providence. All that is created, by the very fact of having been created, belongs to God, its Creator, and consequently, depends on him. In a certain sense every being pertains more 'to God' than 'to itself.' It is first 'of God' and then 'of itself.'"

As Scripture states in Psalms 145:5; 6,7,9, 15-16 and Psalm 104:14-15, God in his divine Providence of the world is the supreme authority over it, full of compassion for all creatures, and especially for human beings.

Divine Providence as relayed by Pope John Paul II: "Divine Providence bears perfect witness to the mystery of the Father, a mystery of Providence and of parental care which embraces every creature, even the most insignificant, like the grass of the field or the sparrows as mentioned in Matthew 6:31-33 and Luke 12:29-31. How much more, therefore, human beings! Christ especially wished to emphasize this. If divine Providence is so generous in regard to creatures inferior to man, how much more will it have care for him!"

[Pope John Paul, speaking of the wisdom of God and His Divine Providence, tells us that all that God has created He does preserve, and we find this message of the preservation of finality in the renewal of all creatures through the redeemed of man as mentioned in Romans 8:19-23. — MBP]

Pope John Paul II states: "The Apostle Paul wrote: 'He is the image of the invisible God, the first-born of all creation; for in him all things were created.' (Colossians 1:15-16) Thus, the word created in Christ the eternal Son, bears in itself from the beginning as the first gift of Providence, the call, or the pledge of predestination in Christ. The finality of the world is joined to this, as the fulfillment of the definite eschatological (end time) salvation, and first of all of humanity. *'For in him [Christ] all the fullness of God was pleased to dwell.'* (Colossians 1:19) The fulfillment of the finality of the world, and especially of man, takes place precisely by means for this fullness which is in Christ. Christ is the fullness. That finality of the world is fulfilled in him in a certain sense. According to it, divine Providence cares for and governs the things of the world, and in particular, man in the world, his life and his history."

The Pope says Divine Providence is expressed in the attainment of the end which correspond to the eternal plan of salvation. "God wants everyone to be saved and reach full knowledge of the truth. (1 Tim. 2:4) In this process, thanks to the 'fullness' of Christ, in him and through him, sin is overcome. Speaking of the fullness which has taken up its abode in Christ, the Apostle proclaimed: *For in him all the fullness of God was pleased to dwell, and through him to reconcile to himself all things, whether on earth or in heaven, making peace by the blood of his cross.* (Colossians 1)

[The Pope states that sin is opposed to the end-times restoration of creation. Sin will be defeated when Jesus returns and Satan and his demons will be sent into the abyss. — MBP]

Pope John Paul II states that God does not will evil as such, yet God, having given man a free will, permits evil. But as the Book of Wisdom says, *God did not make death, and he does not delight in the death of the living. For he created all things that they may exist.* (Wisdom

1:13-14) God permits evil for the overall good of the material cosmos (the restoration of the physical world).

In conclusion, the Pope says the truth about divine Providence, about God's transcendent government of the created world, becomes intelligible (understood) in the light of the truth about the kingdom of God, about the kingdom which God has eternally intended to realize in the created world on the basis of the "predestination in Christ" who is "the first-born of all creation." (Colossians 1:15)

The Pope left the following message for man to internalize concerning animals and the Holy Spirit in 1990: "Animals possess a soul and men must love and feel solidarity with our smaller brethren." He said that all animals are "fruit of the creative action of the Holy Spirit and merit respect." He went on to say that they are "as near to God as men are."

The Life of Pope John Paul II

Pope John Paul II was born Karol Wojtyla on May 18, 1920, in Wadowica, Poland. He had two older siblings who died in infancy. He had an older brother, Edmund. Edmund was very intelligent and earned the degree of Medical Science in 1930. Young Karol was very close to his brother and would visit him often at the hospital where Edmund worked. While his brother was a doctor at the Municipal hospital in Bielsko, Karol would put on one-man shows to entertain the patients.

Tragedy plagued the family, as his mother died when Karol was about eight. And four years later, his brother Edmund, who had great compassion for the sick and because he treated many diseased with scarlet fever whom other doctors would not treat, he himself caught scarlet fever and died in 1932 at the age of twenty-six.

His father was a professional lieutenant for the District of

Wadowice in Poland. His father raised him and they were very close, often going on pilgrimages and enriching their Christian faith and deep desire to follow God. His father had very strict rules; however, he also allowed his son about two hours of play after school, and then young Karol did his homework, followed most often by a walk with his father in the evening. Karol was a very good student and a leader of various organizations.

As a child, Karol Wojtyla loved theater and acted in many productions. He studied literature and drama in Krakow. He and some friends founded the student theater group "Studio 39" in 1939. For a time he was in the military service. Soon after he went back into public life, his father died, leaving young Karol with no immediate family. He prayed beside his father's body for more than a day in his deep sorrow.

Karol lived through the Nazi occupation and for a time was forced to go underground when the Nazis invaded. He was to be saved by hiding in the archbishop's palace. During this time he worked in a stone quarry and a chemical plant while studying secretly for the priesthood.

As a young man, he liked literature and excelled in several foreign languages as a student. He learned to speak seven languages fluently. This has helped him greatly in communication of the Gospel throughout the world. He played soccer and enjoyed canoeing and other sports in his youth and adulthood as well.

Karol had a close friend in his youth who was Jewish. His friend lost his family in the concentration camps. This left a life-long impact on Karol and led him to profess love, resolution without war, and the relentless pursuit of communications with all religions of the world. His writings state that he has never wavered from stating that man is saved by grace alone and that only through the blood of Jesus Christ, the redemption of our souls. But he very strongly believed one should keep the door open to communicate with others of all religions and creeds in the hope that love will prevail and the message of Christ will go forth.

In 1946 he became a priest and went on to earn a doctorate in theology in Rome. He also taught social ethics at the Krakow seminary from 1952-1958. He became archbishop in 1964 and was elected Pope in 1978 at age 58, changing his name to Pope John Paul II. He was known as a very outdoorsy priest, with a love for God's creation, sports, and people, especially young people. Quoted by Pope John Paul II in a prayer at St. Peter's, Philadelphia, in 1979: "What really matters in life is that we are loved by Christ, and that we love Him in return. In comparison to the love of Jesus, everything else is secondary. And without the love of Jesus, everything else is useless."

He focused heavily on reforming the second Vatican Council, including more compassion for humans and animals alike. He put much emphasis on following Scripture and speaking out against abortion and homosexuality. He has had a greater influence on the Catholic faith than any Pope before him making thousands of public appearances, traveling all over the world and meeting with huge audiences everywhere he has gone. His message is that while God rules over all, it is only through professed faith in Jesus Christ as Savior that those calling themselves Christians can spend eternity in heaven. Mike Towle, in his book, *The Quotable John Paul II*, says, "Pope John Paul is born-again Christian as much as he is pope."

John Paul II died on April 2, 2005, after serving twenty-eight years as Pope.

CHAPTER 9

Saint Francis of Assisi, The Patron Saint of Animals

References:

- ❧ The Life of St. Francis of Assisi, taken from www.shrinesf.org
- ❧ David Burr, translator, *Concerning St. Francis of Assisi and the Animals*
- ❧ Elizabeth Goudge, *My God and My All*

Saint Francis of Assisi was a Catholic monk who had a most intimate relationship with God and the creatures of earth. Much has been written about him and the Catholic Church has a special day dedicated to Saint Francis. Saint Francis so loved the animals and his Lord he was inspired to create the first nativity scene. We have continued to create nativity scenes every year to celebrate the birth of Jesus.

Saint Francis, who always referred to the animals as his brothers and sisters, was known for his love for animals. The following stories are for the most part about birds. It is true that birds have a much higher intelligence than we recognize and they seem attracted to hearing human voices and music. Birds were brought into the temples in Solomon's day and sang along with the music played for the religious services.

[When I was growing up there was a Christian radio program broadcast out of Iowa and they had canaries that sang along with the hymns every Sunday. In 1998 I was invited to give a talk for the annual Blessing of the Animals Day at the Noah's Ark Pet Cemetery in Grand Rapids, Michigan. Before the event I attended the nearby Church of Christ's open-air service, which they hold once a year in

Grand Rapids. To my amazement, when the congregation started singing a hymn of praise, I looked above me and an entire flock of birds continually circled the congregation, chirping at the tops of their voices until the end of the hymn, and at which time they promptly flew away. I felt that I had just received a tremendous blessing from nature only God could provide.

I had a devoted Christian nephew in Alaska who would go out into the woods near his home and sit down, and the wild animals, even natural enemies, would come and sit beside him. His mother said it was a most amazing sight. They would sit together for long periods of time and then all leave. He died when he was twenty-one years old of a strange illness in which blood seeps into the lungs.

Thus it is not hard for me to understand that animals do quite often respond to certain people to whom God has given a special talent and gift of communication with nature. I do not say that animals, including birds, truly understand much of anything we say, but more likely they can look into the soul and spirit of man in a way only God understands. Saint Francis had the gift of praising God with the birds and it is told that he met a vicious wolf that was obedient to him also. The stories concerning Saint Francis are considered fables to some and to others true stories. I believe from my own experiences that there is truth in his ability to reach out to them on a spiritual level that most of us cannot. These are stories to contemplate and stories many expect to be included in such a book as this so I will pass on some of the stories told of him. — MBP]

Saint Francis was passing through the valley of Spoleto with Angelo and Masseo, fellow brothers in the Lord. When he came to a field as they walked toward Bevagna, they discovered a flock of birds. They were all very happy enjoying the benefits of the harvest field with water and trees nearby. Francis rejoiced as he observed the eager little creatures, and their joyous chattering voices gave him great delight. He loved the creatures and had the gift of winning their trust and friendship, and seeing the birds delighting in the bounty of God touched his heart deeply and he simply could not journey on, leaving them without speaking to them as only Saint Francis could. He told his companions to wait for him while he ministered to the birds. He thus went into the field where the birds were all about him on the ground, and to his delight they were not frightened of him. The ones on the ground stayed where they were, even though his habit touched them as he moved gently among them. He talked to them and when they heard his voice the ones in the trees came flying down and settled themselves around him. Francis said to them, "My little sisters the birds, ye owe much to God, your Creator, and ye ought to sing His praises at all times and in all places, because He has given you liberty to fly about into all places. And though ye neither spin nor sew, He has given you a twofold and threefold clothing for yourselves and for your offspring. Two of all your species He sent into the ark with Noah that you might not be lost to the world; besides which, He feeds you, though ye neither sow nor reap. He has given you fountains and rivers to quench your thirst, mountains and valleys in which you take refuge and trees in which to build your nests! So that your Creator loves you much, having thus favored you with such bounties. Beware, my little sisters, of the sin of ingratitude, and study always to give praise to God." As he said these words, all the birds began to open their beaks, to stretch their necks, to spread their wings, and reverently to bow their heads to the ground, endeavoring by their motions and by their songs to manifest their joy to Saint Francis. And the Saint rejoiced with them. He wondered to see such a multitude of birds, and was charmed with their beautiful variety, with their attention and familiarity, for all of which he devoutly gave thanks to the Creator. As he finished addressing his feathery sisters the birds, Saint Francis made the sign of the cross, and gave them leave to fly away. Then all the birds rose up into the air, singing most sweetly following the sign of the cross, which Saint Francis had made. They divided themselves into four companies; one company toward the east, another toward the west, one toward the south, and one toward the north, each company as it went singing most wonderfully.

Saint Francis and his companions agree in reporting. Rejoicing, the blessed father went off with his companions, giving thanks to God whom all creatures worship. Since he had now been made simple by grace and not by nature, he began to accuse himself of negligence for not having ministered to the birds before, since they listened to the word of God with such reverence. And thus it came about that, from that day on, he exhorted all birds, all animals, all reptiles, and even nonexistent creatures to praise and love the creator, for every day, when the name of the savior was announced, he himself saw their obedience.

One day Saint Francis came to a town called Alviano to preach the word of God. Ascending to where he could be seen by all, he asked for silence. The people became quiet and waited reverently, but a flock of swallows building nests nearby were excitedly chattering away, making it impossible for the people to hear. Francis spoke to them, "My sisters the swallows, it's my turn to speak now, because you've already said enough. Listen to the word of God. Stay still and be quiet until it's over." To the people's amazement, the little birds immediately stopped chattering and did not move until Francis had finished preaching. Those who witnessed this sign were filled with wonder and said, "Truly this man is holy and a friend of the Most High." Praising and blessing God, they devoutly hurried to touch his clothing. To those observing it was truly miraculous to witness what seemed to them irrational creatures recognizing Saint Francis' affection for them and sensed his love.

Saint Francis loved all animals, especially birds, and his favorite was the lark because the sister lark had a cowl like a religious. The killing of birds most horrified him and he tried to get the Emperor to pass a law that no man would be allowed to kill a lark or harm them in any way. And he wanted a law passed that all animals, including birds, would be fed on Christmas Day.

Once, when he was staying in the town of Greccio, a levert [hare or rabbit] was caught in a trap and brought live to Francis by a brother. Seeing the levert, the blessed man was moved to pity and said, "Brother Hare, come here. Why did you let yourself be fooled in this way?" As soon as the hare was released by the brother he dashed over to Francis and, without being forced to do so, settled into his lap as the safest place available. When he had rested there a while, the Holy Father, stroking him with maternal affection, let him go so that he could return to the wild. Each time he was placed on the ground, the hare ran back to Francis' lap. Finally, Francis asked that the brothers carry him to a nearby forest. Something similar occurred with another rabbit, a very undomesticated creature, on an island in the lake of Perugia.

There was one very funny story about Saint Francis. He and eleven brothers returned to Assisi, where they had managed to construct a form of hut in the hills near the city in which to live and pray. Saint Francis and his brothers went back to the hut to live but it was not to long until they had a most unusual guest. The guest arrived in the form of a donkey, a wonderful and humble symbol of creation, such as the one that carried Mary to the birthing place of our Lord and Savior. As the story goes, Saint Francis and his brothers were praying when suddenly in the doorway of their hut appeared the head and shoulders of a donkey. Then came the words "Get in with you, get well within, for we shall do well within this place." Following behind the ass was a most ill-mannered peasant bringing up the rear. Saint Francis was quick to conclude that there was not enough room for the twelve of them as well as a donkey and a man, as the latter had no intention of leaving, so the brothers picked up their meager belongings and went to find a cave to stay in.

Now without even a roof over their heads, Saint Francis felt led to go to Bishop Guido to see if there was any help he could offer, but the Bishop could not help him this time. Saint Francis, remembering the wonderful Abbey on the mountain, climbed up to the

Benedictine Abbey. There he met with the Abbot who gladly offered the brother the property of Portiuncula. Yet as wonderful as that was, Francis immediately knew he could not accept any property. That problem was quickly rectified when the Abbot said he would rent the property and dwellings to the brothers for the price of one basket of fish per year caught in the river. Each year the twelve brothers gave the Abbot one basket of fish, and the Abbot would send a receipt of payment in the shape of a vessel of oil. Now the brothers had a place to sleep and pray. They could plant vegetables, grow fruit trees and plant beautiful flowers.

Saint Francis believed in constant prayer and living a sacrificial life for Christ and living in complete obedience. He was a very gentle leader to Christian brothers in the faith; however, he would become extremely angry if any of the brothers were in any way disobedient to the faith.

The Life of Saint Francis ofr Assisi

Francis was born in 1182, the oldest son of a wealthy cloth merchant and a mother of royal heritage, in central Italy. Francis enjoyed a life of luxury with the finest of clothes, fun-loving friends for whom he was a leader, and totally experienced the life of ease. He loved playing the violin and singing with his friends. However, there were poor and starving people all around in the streets, alleys, and countryside of Assisi where he lived. The poor and diseased were considered unworthy of help in the society of the day, so he was brought up without any real concern for them.

But when he was sixteen he began to have a change of heart. One beggar had asked him for anything he might give, but Francis initially refused to give him anything and the beggar went away. However, within a few minutes, Francis had a change of heart and ran out into the street and found the man and gave him some money. Francis could no longer bear to see the hungry and homeless without food and clothing. He started giving away his clothes and any money he had. Finally, his father became furious about his generosity. As he reached the age of about twenty, with his father completely disagreeing about concerns for the needy, Francis felt led to take a vow of poverty, living only on what he could earn or beg for. This was the last straw. His father demanded that he repay the money he had been given and had given away, which Francis did.

Francis was committed to a life of poverty but it was a struggle for him. He slept in caves, worked at anything he could for food, and begged when no food was available to eat. He would not take any money for work or alms. But as time went on, others could see his heart and commitment to God and his love for the lepers whom everyone shunned.

Saint Francis learned to love and care for the lepers of the area, and there were many. He and his fellow brothers started ministering to them on a continuous basis. Saint Francis started making the sign of the cross also, which was to protect him from injury, disease or any harm that might befall him and his fellow brothers.

Eventually others, many of rich and of royal background, came to join him and take the vow of poverty. When the little group reached twelve members, they decided to go to Rome and establish a new order, "The Brothers Minor." Though Pope Innocent III first rejected his plea for a new order, through divine intervention the Pope gave permission for the new order to be officially established. The new order of poverty, "The Brothers Minor," was later to be known as the Franciscans.

Toward the end of his life, the order was changing. Some of the new brothers wanted some comforts that had not been allowed and this saddened Saint Francis greatly. Saint Francis suffered in sickness for almost ten years and was ready to go home to be with his Lord and Savior. His brothers had aided him during his long sickness for which he felt badly and had physically suffered much. He asked his doctor if he had much longer and when he learned he would soon be going home to be with Jesus he made some special requests for his departure from earth and entry into his heavenly home. He sent a messenger to Rome to request Lady Giacoma to come to him and bring a gray gown, a napkin for his face, a cushion for his head, wax candles, and an almond sweet cake. When she and her sons arrived, the porter came running to Saint Francis saying that no woman was allowed on the property, and asking how this problem should be solved. Thus Saint Francis said to bring "Brother Giacoma" to us. Lady Giacoma came, bringing the items requested. She had had a dream that she was to hasten to Saint Francis, as he was to die on Saturday. No doubt he did get to enjoy his almond sweet cake, and for his funeral he was dressed in the gray habit she had woven for him, the pillow she made supporting his head, and the candles burning around him as the people passed by his coffin. He was buried in a grave in San Giorgio, the church where he had learned his lessons as a child and preached his first sermon. Clare, the first female nun of the order and dear friend of Saint Francis, and her sister had one last look at her beloved friend as the brothers carried the bier into the chapel and brought it to the grille behind which Clare and her sister were waiting. They brought the body up over the iron grating and Clare viewed her beloved friend one last time on this earth. Saint Francis of Assisi passed on to eternal life in 1228 at the age of forty-six.

CHAPTER 10

Martin Luther, Protestant Reformer and Founder of the Lutheran Church

References:

- Lectures from his original works and his writings on the Book of Romans
- *Love For Animals* by Dix Harwood
- *Luther's Works,* Volume 25 and Volume 46
- *Lectures on Romans* edited by Hilton C. Oswald
- *The Christian in Society* edited by Robert C. Schultz
- Interview with Concordia Seminary students
- *Life of Luther* edited by Gustave Just

Martin Luther's doctrines became the foundation upon which mainstream Protestant and non-denominational Christian churches were founded. This was not his intention or his decision. It resulted from his exploration of biblical truths and the encouragement and support of fellow priests and monks. Martin Luther believed in the immortality of animals, but also believed that they were primarily for the use of man as he saw fit.

In *Love for Animals* by Dix Harwood, a story is recounted that a little girl named Thekla, who was heartbroken over the death of her little dog, came to Martin Luther to be comforted. She asked him a most disturbing theological question. "Will Nix rise again at the last day?" she asked. "Will there be dogs in the other world?" The listeners surrounding Luther trembled at such blasphemy, as they considered it. But it was spoken from the innocent lips of a child who could realize no difference between a friend with two legs and one with four. The listeners gasped and exchanged glances, concerned with the relative value of faith and works or any doctrine concerning such a subject. But Luther was undisturbed as he smiled at the grieving little girl.

"We know less of what that other world is like," said he, "than this little one knows of the empires or powers of this world. But of this we are sure, the world to come will be no empty, lifeless waste... God will make a new heaven and a new earth. All poisonous and malicious and hurtful creatures will be banished there, all that our sin has ruined. All creatures will not only be harmless, but lovely and joyful, so that we might play with them. The suckling child shall play on the hole of the asp, and the weaned child shall put his hand on the cockatrice's den. Why, then, should there not be little dogs in the new earth, whose skin might be as fair as gold, and their hair as bright as precious stones?"

[Luther understood life as God created it in Genesis before the fall of man when all creatures lived in perfect harmony, none destroying each other, in an eternal state, and understood as well Isaiah 11:6-9, in which once again all creation will be at peace. All creation will be restored to its perfection as before the fall. The audience was most appalled at the question Thekla asked Martin Luther. At that time in history, animal immortality was ignored by most Christians, both Catholic and Protestant. And in that era the wealthy were considered more righteous, as God must look with favor on them due to their blessed life of wealth and honor. Even slaves and very low-income people and particularly those in prison due to lack of ability to pay their debts were considered not fit to enter heaven. So the idea of animals in heaven would certainly make many feel their social position or importance in the sight of God was threatened. — MBP]

Luther also said there would be a new heaven and new earth, as the apostle Peter said that in the last day there would be a restoration of all things when God creates a new heaven and a new earth, and even a little dog like Nix will also be created new. He said, "All creatures will not only be harmless, but lovely and joyful." He quoted the following scriptures from the Apostle John: *And God shall wipe away all tears from their eyes; and there shall be no more death, neither sorrow, nor crying, neither shall there be any more pain: for the former things are passed away.* (Revelation 21:4 KJV) *He that overcometh shall inherit all things; and I will be his God, and he shall be my son.* (Revelation 21:7 KJV)

Luther's position and biblical understanding of an afterlife for animals was foreign to the mindset of the day. However, by the mid-eighteenth century, English Christians did humble themselves to discussing the afterlife of animals without seeming blasphemous.

In speaking concerning Genesis, Luther stated that animals were subordinate to human beings. Man is the only being created in the image of God, but is not the only part of creation to glorify God. He stated that man was the noblest of all the animals; however, he did acknowledge that the lower creatures are the "footprints of God."

Luther, in accord with Solomon's writing in Ecclesiastes, says that humans after the fall of man could no longer understand the disposition of the animals.

[The companionship man and animals shared had now been separated by the sins of man. Adam had named the animals. They had been man's helpmates, they could communicate with Adam. They were all going to physically live forever but then man sinned. — MBP]

Luther said that God decided to destroy both evil man and animals yet He preserved some of the animals in a gracious gesture to serve man's purpose. Until the flood, he said, no animals were eaten but after the flood man was given divine permission to eat animals. Now, they have to endure "a more oppressive form of bondage" and human beings exercise "a more extensive and oppressive dominion." The animals are subjected to man as to a tyrant who has absolute power over life and earth. Yet even though this power is absolute, it is not arbitrary. "God wants not even an animal killed except in a just manner, that is either for sacrifice or for human consumption. He believed that even though animals were to be killed and eaten it would not always be so in the new heaven and new earth and the original harmony between man and animals will be restored.

[One comment Luther made is partially true; however, to say that God preserved the animals for humans is scripturally unsound. God created the non-human world for Himself and He has and will use them to destroy the wicked. — MBP]

Luther spoke on Deuteronomy 22:6 concerning the treatment of animals, which forbids the harming of the mother bird if her eggs or chicks are gathered up. Luther wrote, "What else does this law teach but that by the kind treatment of animals they are to learn gentleness and kindness?" *If a bird's nest chance to be before thee in the way in any tree, or on the ground, whether they be young ones, or eggs, and the dam sitting upon the young, or upon the eggs, thou shalt not take the dam with the young.* (Deuteronomy 22:6 KJV)

Luther stated that because animals were not created in God's image they lacked the ability to be rational. Yet they should have a form of dignity and concern. God promises to redeem and renew, so they can be expected to share in the restitution of all things. He believed that our mistreatment of animals will have eternal significance; because, he says, as with the survival of all our victims in a redeemed creation, their presence and "forgiveness" will be for us a kind of judgment.

In his sermon "Keeping Children in School," speaking of the education of children, the future of the world, world government and the laws that protect man and which man is to follow, is a gift from God for man alone. The animals do not have this gift, this ability. But if they did, Luther states, "Do you not think that if the birds and the beasts were to see the worldly government that exists among men they would say—if they could speak—'O men! Compared with us you are not men but gods! What security you have, both you and your possessions, while among us no one is safe from another regarding life, home, or food, supply, not even for a moment!' Shame upon your ingratitude—you do not even see what a splendid life the God of us all has given you compared with us beasts!"

Luther said all estates and works of God are to be praised as highly as they can be, and none despised in favor of another. For it is written, *What God does is fine and beautiful, and none despised in favor of another.* (Psalm 104:31) God rejoices in his works (creation). Luther also asked "How many people has God put on earth who misuse all His kindness and all His creatures?"

Matthew Henry, in his commentary, repeats "God always rejoices in his works (all creation). It shall endure to the end of time in his works of creation and providence; it shall endure to eternity in the happiness and adoration of saints and angels. Man's glory is fading; God's glory is everlasting. God always rejoices in His works because they are all done in wisdom."

[Luther says that the animals will be used as instruments of God in punishing the wicked of the earth. This is a fact we have overwhelming evidence of through biblical scriptures dealing both with the past as recorded by the prophets and what no doubt will happen in the future as recorded in the Book of Revelation. — MBP]

Luther lectures on I Corinthians 15

For Christ will be king until he has defeated all his enemies, including the last enemy—death. This too must be defeated and ended. For the rule and authority over all things has been given to Christ by his Father; except, of course, Christ does not rule over the Father himself, who gave him this power to rule. (1 Corinthians 15:25-27 TLB)

1 Corinthians 15:35-45 explains the essence of a natural body of flesh and blood as opposed to spiritual bodies. If there is a body of flesh and blood, a physical body, there is also a spiritual body. Whether they be human, animal, or even plants, all flesh must die and go into the ground as seed to come up as a new kind of body, a

new eternal body. Luther speaks of Spirit given to redeemed man stating that they are born-again into a new life, adopted into the family of God.

Luther explains that a body such as is born on earth, which for its natural preservation or sustenance requires meat and drink, clothing, fire, water, air, and other fleshly needs, just as a beastly body; thus we are very little different than the animals. He says the only difference is that animals cannot reason.

Animals were created to serve man to the point of being sacrificed for their welfare and in this manner they carry out a Christlike function for the sake of the sinful and endangered species, man.

Luther writes about how foolish it is for us to try to understand God and His creation from a human point of view, and how philosophy rather than Scripture clouds the truth and leads to misguided assertions and theology.

Luther states, "The expectation of the creature, by virtue of the fact that God has the power of hearing the creature waiting, he no longer directs his inquiry toward the creature as such but to what it waits for (eternal bliss). But alas, how deeply and painfully we are caught up in categories and the understanding of what makes something what it is leading to the folly of opinions not worthy of our time." Luther states: "We do not know what we should know because we have learned superfluous things; indeed, we do not know what is good for us because we have learned only what harms us.

"For I consider that the sufferings, that is, the tribulations, of this present time, as if he were saying: 'of this brief and limited period,' are not worth, as indeed they really are not worth, comparing with the glory which already has been prepared by God but is not yet revealed, that is to be revealed in us, who are the elect.

"(19) For the expectation, because it is in captivity and slavery to the unworthy of the creation, that is, the structure, the fabric, which makes up the whole world, waits for, longs for, the revealing, in the resurrection and glorification, of the sons of God, and so it is.

Why do you say it is awaiting it?"

"To suffer with" is usually taken in the sense of "to feel pity," but there it is taken in the sense of "suffering together" with Christ, that is, suffering the same things that Christ suffered.

Paul is speaking of creation, as if it were feeling, living, and suffering. It has long been compelled to serve the ungodly (humanity) in their abuse and their ingratitude to God, although it (creation/creatures) is created so that through it and in it God may be glorified by His saints. Therefore it (all creation) quite naturally is awaiting this its end.

Heaven and earth will pass away (Matthew 24:35), not as far as the substance (the physical heaven and earth) is concerned, but with regard to corruptibility. I do not interpret this of the substance (not that they should no longer exist but that they should no longer be subject to corruption but be glorious.) For the world "will pass away" suggests that they will be changed. Just as Christ made a change in His Passover, that is, was changed.

(20) For the creation was subjected to futility, that is, to the vain use of the ungodly, that is, it is enslaved, not of its own will, not of its own desire, but of necessity, but by the will of Him, God, who subjected it in hope, that is, made it subject to the unworthy. (21) Because the creation itself, Matt. 24: 35 "heaven and earth will pass away," will be set free from its bondage to decay, under which it serves corruptibly, into an incorruptible service, indeed, into liberty, into the glorious liberty, that is, into the glory, of the children of God, because this service will be actually His liberty, just as also the righteous can be said to have been delivered from the bondage of sin into the service of righteousness, or rather, into the liberty of righteousness. Because to serve God is to rule. (22) For we know that the whole creation, for "all things work together for them who are the elect," as we read below (Romans 8:28) has been groaning, for the redemption of the glory of the children of God and of itself, in travail, but has not yet brought forth, until now. (23) And not only the

creation, which is not in the Greek, but we ourselves, the believers, the elect, who have the firstfruits of the Spirit. We do not yet possess the fullness and the creation" (James 1:18). But in the future we shall be perfect according to 1 John 3:2: "We are God's children now; it does not yet appear what we shall be, but we know within ourselves, where no one sees us except God, we pray in our groaning and hope as we wait, with a longing for the life to come and a weariness for the present life, for the adoption as sons of God, the redemption of our body, from mortality to immortality, from corruption to glory. (24) For in this hope, "in which we are waiting," we were saved, with an eternal salvation. Now hope, the thing which through hope is waited for, that is seen is not hope, and he explains himself thus: for what a man sees, why does he hope for it? Because he already has and holds it. (25) But if we hope for what we do not see, and do not have and hold, we wait for it with patience, for hope which is deferred afflicts the soul. (26). Likewise the Spirit, the Holy Spirit, helps, with deep groaning and intercession, our weakness, our infirmity, our lack of strength (the Greek has "our weaknesses"), for we do not know what, so far as what we ask in concerned, we should pray for as we ought, so far as the state of mind or the manner of our prayer is concerned, as we read in Matthew. 20:22, "You do not know what you are asking," and John 13:7, "What I am doing you do not know now," (27) but the Spirit Himself, the Holy Spirit, intercedes, makes intercession, for us with sighs too deep for words, which cannot be expressed in words by any man, nor can anyone perceive them but only God. (The spirit intercedes, makes intercession, for the saints according to the will of God,) Because he has said that the whole creation and we ourselves and the Spirit sigh for the saints, he proves it by saying: (28). We know, I say, I assert, that the Spirit Himself intercedes, lest this seem strange, that all things, both good as well as evil, work for good, that is, for the increase of salvation, for those who love Him, who are called according to His purpose, according to His predestination, for not all are called according to the predestination, because "many are called, but few are chosen."

He uses the term "according to purpose" in an absolute sense, not adding "God's" or "His," For there really is only one purpose, namely, God's, as they who understand God know. For the purpose of no one else is accomplished except who understand God know. For the purpose of no one else is accomplished except that of God, to whom every creature is conformed. *Let all Thy creatures serve thee.* (Judith 16:14)

(30) And those whom He predestined, proposed or chose, He also called, to faith through the Word, and those whom He called He also justified, through the Spirit of faith, and those whom He justified He also magnified, in place of "glorified," that is, He glorified them in eternal life. (31) What then shall we say, as it is as if he was saying: "Nothing," to this? In opposition to those points which are so immutable. If God, He Himself, the very Judge of all men, it is for us, not our innocent life or the virtue of our righteousness, but He who can do all things and performs all things who is against us? For the whole creation is obedient to the Creator. Will He not give us all things with Him. It is as if he were saying that it is impossible for Him not to, since in His Son He has made and holds all things. "Upholding all things by the Word of His power" (Hebrews 1:3)

The apostle is therefore right when, in Col. 2:8, he speaks up against philosophy and says: "Beware lest any man cheat you by philosophy and vain deceit according to the tradition of men." If the apostle Paul had wanted to understand any philosophy as something good and useful, he certainly would not have condemned it so unequivocally! We conclude, therefore, "that anyone who searches into the essence and functioning's of the creatures rather than into their sightings and earnest expectations is certainly foolish and blind. He does not know that also the creatures are created for an end. This passage shows this clearly enough."

For the creature was made subject to vanity, not willingly, but by reason of him that made it subject, in hope. (Romans 8:20) Most interpreters take the term "creature" in this passage to mean man, because he has a share in everything created. But it is better to understand man through the word "vanity," as it says expressly and very rightly in Ps. 39:5: *Surely every man living is altogether vanity.* For it is certainly true that, if man, the old man, were not, there would be no vanity. For all that God made "was very good" (Gen.1:31) and is good to this day, as the apostle says in I Tim.4:4: *Every creature of God is good,* and in Titus 1:15: *To the pure all things are pure.* It therefore becomes vain, evil, and noxious, etc., without its fault and from the outside, namely, in this way: Because man does not judge and evaluate it rightly and because he enjoys it in a wrong way, he regards it more highly than fact and truth allow, inasmuch as man who is able to grasp God and to find his fulfillment in God alone (as far as his mind and spirit are concerned) presumes to possess this peace and satisfaction in created things. It is to this vanity, therefore (i.e., to this wrong enjoyment), that the creature is subjected, just as grass is in itself something good and not something worthless; indeed, it is good, necessary, and useful to cattle, but to man it is worthless and useless as a food, yet if it were used as human food, it would be regarded and valued more highly than its nature allows. So do all who do not love God from a really pure heart and who do not fervently thirst for him. This is characteristic of every man who is born of Adam and lives without the Holy Spirit. Hence, it is said of all in Ps. 13:3: "They are all gone aside," i.e., they have become vain. And through man the whole creature becomes vanity, though, to be sure, against its will. As the Preacher says: "Vanity of vanities, and all is vanity. What has a man more (than vanity) of all his labor that he takes under the sun?" (Eccl. 1:2 ff.) He says significantly that man has no other profit than vanity. For created things are good in themselves, and those who know God know also the things of nature not as something vain but as they are in truth; and they use them but do not take advantage of them. Hence, it says in Titus 1:15, "To the pure all things are pure," but to the impure nothing is pure. So then, the same things are pure and impure on account of the fact that they to whom they are either pure or impure differ from one another.

Because the creature also itself shall be delivered from the servitude of corruption into the liberty of the glory of the children of God. For we know that every creature groans and travails in pain, even till now. And not only it, but ourselves also, who have the first fruits of the Spirit, even we ourselves groan within ourselves, waiting for the adoption of the sons of God, the redemption of our body. (Rom. 8:21-23)

As scripture says, *We look for a new heaven and new earth* (II Peter 3:13); *For, behold, I create new heavens and a new earth* (Isaiah 65:17); *They shall perish... and thou shalt change them, and they shall be changed."* (Psalms 102:26-27)

[Psalms 102 says they shall perish and then be changed. "Perish" plainly does not mean annihilation. — MBP]

Again Luther contrasts "the bondage of corruption" and "the liberty of glory," for it now serves in its corruption to the misuse of the wicked, but then, when it will be set free from corruption, it will serve "to the glory of the children of God."

Notice what a great prayer is continuously said for the righteous and again the unrighteous, as the whole creature groans for its own deliverance and that if the righteous, thereby crying out against the unrighteous; then we come and groan, and finally also the Sprit himself. "It (creation) travails," i.e., it strives anxiously for the end of corruption, in order to bring forth glory.

He says two things: First, the creature will be delivered, namely, from vanity, when the wicked will have been damned and taken away and the old man abolished. Such deliverance happens even now every day in the saints. Second, it will also no longer be either vain or corruptible. Hence, the saying of (Isaiah. 30:26): *And the light of the moon shall be as the light of the sun, and the light of the sun shall be sevenfold, as the light of seven days.*

[Luther did believe that any unnecessary killing of animals has never been sanctified by God. He says: "The arbitrary killing of animals is not sanctioned. Humans must still act prudently even when confronted by 'wild beasts.' These wild beasts are God's agents of wrath against human wickedness, and a sign of God's perfect rule over the creation in which human beings exercise a defective dominion." Clearly animals have a distinctive role to play, says Luther, in the creation which awaits its ultimate fulfillment. Even dangerous animals are "'sacred" (especially?) when they threaten. — MBP]

Luther sums up his understanding of heaven in saying that in Paradise there was complete harmony between man and animals, due to the fall, all was corrupted and disrupted but one day again that harmony will be restored and all creation will be made anew as Christ will be in all and all in all.

> "Our Lord has written the promise of the resurrection
> not in books alone, but in every leaf in the springtime."
> — Martin Luther

The Life of Martin Luther

Martin Luther was born in Eisleben, Germany, in November 1483 and died in February 1546 at the age of 63. He was raised Roman Catholic, went through his elementary and secondary school and university in Catholic schools, having to help earn his own way in his earlier education, as his parents were peasants making a sufficient living but not enough to provide a quality education for their son. His father did eventually make a much better living as part owner of some coal mines after being a coal miner all of his life. There were at least nine children in the Luther family, Martin being the oldest. The father was very strict and Martin received many beatings through his young life.

Luther was by nature a very happy and positive person, even though he was schooled away from home in a strict and harsh environment from an early age. In his youth he never escaped strict and harsh punishment for deeds he did and did not do. Luther's father recognized a great intelligence in his son and did save every cent he could to further his son's education. He was the youngest monk to be made Doctor of Divinity because of his great learning abilities and understanding of Scripture. Though he first studied law, he studied diligently trying to learn the laws of God through obedience to the church and its teachings. It was while at the University at the age of seventeen that he found a Bible to read and as a student of earnest searching, read to learn all the things of God he could digest.

When Luther first became a monk and entered the cloister he felt his work for God would be pleasing to God, but no matter what he did, how much he prayed, and what sacrifices he made he could not find any peace. Dr. Staupitz, who knew Luther had a genuine desire to know the word, released him from the menial labors and encouraged him to continue in the diligent study of Holy Scriptures. One day Staupitz found Luther in great distress of spirit and said to him, "Ah, you do not know how beneficial and necessary such trials are for you; without them nothing good would become of you. For God does not send them to you in vain. You will see that He will use you for great things." And later when Staupitz heard Luther say "Oh my sin, my sin, my sin!" Staupitz told him, "Christ is the forgiveness of real sins. He is a real Savior and you are a real sinner. God has sent His own Son and delivered Him up for us." Another time when, because of great anxiety for his sins, he became sick, an old friar comforted him with these words, "I believe in the forgiveness of sin," and explained these words to mean: "It is not enough that you believe that your sins, your sins, your sins are forgiven. For man is justified by grace through faith." At that time, a ray of light fell into Luther's soul and from this time on his favorite passage remained Romans 3:28: *Therefore we conclude, that a man is justified by faith without the deeds of the Law.*

It was at the university that Luther became very ill and was sure he would die. However, an old priest came to him and comforted him with these prophetic words: "My dear bachelor, be of good cheer. You will not die of this illness. God will yet make a great man of you, who will comfort many people. For whom God loveth and whom He would make a blessing to his fellow men, upon him He early lays the cross; for in the school of affliction patient people learn much."

Luther was to face many trials and personal danger opposing the Pope with his ninety-five "Theses" proposing a discussion of the value of indulgences and became, in a sense, a hunted man by the church leaders. Luther was considered a heretic and attempts were made to have him executed; however, only through the good graces of Elector Frederick the Wise, who had Luther's case tried in Germany, did Luther escape death accused of heresy.

As a monk he became a great minister in ministering the word of salvation to his fellow monks and congregations alike. Dr. Mellrichstadt stated, "That monk will confound all the doctors, and introduce a new doctrine, and reform the whole Roman church, for he devotes himself to the writings of the prophets and apostles, and stands upon the Word of Jesus Christ."

Luther was to translate the Bible to German from Latin, which was a great blessing to the German people. He also contributed great hymns. Among them are "A Mighty Fortress is Our God."

Luther married a Christian lady, Katharine of Bora, and had six children. In 1542 his fourteen-year-old daughter Magdalene became very sick and died. As she came near to death Luther said to his daughter, "Magdalene, my dear little daughter, you would like to remain with this your dear father, wouldn't you, but also gladly go to that Father?" The child answered, "Yes, dear father, as God wills!" She died in his arms on the evening of the twentieth of September. Her mother Katharine was in the room but due to her deep sorrow remained at some distance. At the funeral, though in deep sorrow of flesh, he spoke to those attending the funeral and said, "You ought to rejoice! I have sent a saint to heaven, yes, a living saint. O that we had such a death! Such a death I would accept this moment!"

Luther was not financially well off, and was, in fact, quite poor, but his wife was very frugal. Luther, however, gave a student in need a silver cup that was gilded within because he had no money to give him. He gave even when he had little or no money but God always saw the family through.

There grew a doctrinal dispute in Mansfield, thus Luther was requested to come to settle the disagreement. He left with three of his sons in January 1546. There he preached to many and was able to settle the dispute. He became weak in February and had planned to return home but became gravely ill. A Dr. Jonas treated him for two days, but Luther died February 18, 1546. Just before he died he repeated three times *For God so loved the world, that He gave His only begotten Son, that whosoever believeth in Him should not perish, but have everlasting life,* (John 3:16) and the words of the Sixty-eighth Psalm: *He that is our God, is the God of salvation; and unto God the Lord belong the issues of death.* He then repeated three times, "Father, into Thy hands I commend my spirit, Thou hast redeemed me, Lord, Thou faithful God." He then lay quietly and when Dr. Jonas spoke to him, "Reverend father, are you firmly determined to die upon Christ and the doctrine you have preached?" Upon this Luther answered loud and distinctly: "Yes!" He then turned on his side and fell asleep, entering into eternal rest.

CHAPTER 11

John Calvin, Founder of the Presbyterian Church

References:
- www.historylearningsite.co.uk/calvin.htm
- John Calvin's lectures on the immortality of animals from Romans 8:19-22
- Ford Lewis Battles and Andre Malan Huyg, *Calvin's Comments on Seneca de Clementia*
- Williston Walker, *Great Men of the Christian Church*
- William J. Bouwsma, *John Calvin*

John Calvin, founder of the Presbyterian church, did believe in the immortality of animals and based his belief on Romans 8:19-22. He did, however, believe that man had the right to treat them in any manner he saw fit.

In John Calvin's lecture on Romans 8:19-22 he explains Paul's teaching on the subject of eternal life, concerning both the children of God and the remainder of creation—the animals, plants and inanimate creation as well.

John Calvin's commentary; lectures on Romans 8:19-22

The earnest expectation of the creature waiteth for the manifestation of the sons of God. For the creature was made subject to vanity, not willingly, but by reason of him that subjected it: Yet in hope that the creature itself also shall be delivered from the bondage of corruption, into the glorious liberty of the sons of God. For we know that the whole creation groaneth, and travaileth in pain together until now. (Romans 8:19-22).

Romans 8:19: "For the earnest expectation of the creation," etc. He (Paul) teaches us that there is an example of the patience, to which he had exhorted us, even in mute creatures. For, to omit various interpretations, I understand the passage to have this meaning⁻that there is no element and no part of the world which, being touched as it were, with a sense of its present misery, does not intensely hope for a resurrection. He indeed lays down two things: that all are creatures in distress, and yet that they are sustained by hope. And it hence also appears how immense is the value of eternal glory, that it can excite and draw all things to desire it.

Further, the expression, *expectation expects,* or waits for, though somewhat unusual, yet has a most suitable meaning; for he meant to intimate, that all creatures, seized with great anxiety and held in suspense with great desire, look for that day which shall openly exhibit the glory of the children of God. The revelation of God's children shall be, when we shall be like God, according to what John says, "For though we know that we know that we are now his sons, yet it appears not yet what we shall be." (1 John 3:2)

But I have retained the words of Paul; for bolder than what is meet is the version of Erasmus, "Until the sons of God shall be manifest"; nor does it sufficiently express the meaning of the Apostle; for he means not that the sons of God shall be manifested in the last day, but that it shall be then made known how desirable and blessed their condition will be, when they shall put off corruption and put on celestial glory. But he ascribes hope to creatures void of reason for this end⁻that the faithful may open their eyes to behold the invisible life, though as yet it lies hid under a mean garb.

Romans 8:20: "For to vanity has the creation," etc. Paul shows the object of expectation from what is of an opposite character; for as creatures, being now subject to corruption, cannot be restored until the sons of God shall be wholly restored; hence they, longing for their renewal, look forward to the manifestation of the celestial kingdom. He says, that they have been subjected to vanity, and for this reason, because they abide not in a constant and durable state, but being as it were evanescent and unstable, they pass away swiftly; for no doubt he sets vanity in opposition to a perfect state.

"Not willing," etc. Since there is no reason in such creatures, their will is to be taken no doubt for their natural inclination, according to which the whole nature of things tends to its own preservation and perfection: whatever then is detained under corruption suffers violence, nature being unwilling and repugnant. But he introduces all parts of the world, by a sort of personification, as being endued with reason; and he does this in order to shame our stupidity, when the uncertain fluctuation of this world, which we see, does not raise our minds to higher things.

"But on account of him," etc. Paul sets before us an example of obedience in all created things, and adds that it springs from hope; for hence comes the alacrity of the sun and moon, and of all the stars in their constant courses, hence is the sedulity (persistence; constant continuation) of the earth's obedience in bringing forth fruits, hence is the unwearied motion of the air, hence is the prompt tendency of flow in water. God has given to everything its charge; and he has not only by a distinct order commanded what he would to be done, but also implanted inwardly the hope of renovation. For in the sad disorder which followed the fall of Adam, the whole machinery of the world would have instantly become deranged, and all its parts would have failed had not some hidden strength supported them. It would have been then wholly inconsistent that the earnest of the spirit should be less efficacious in the children of God than hidden instinct in the lifeless parts of creation. How much so ever then created things do naturally incline another way; yet as it has pleased God to bring them under vanity, they obey his order; and as he has given them a hope of a better condition, with this they sustain themselves, deferring their desire, until the incorruption promised to them shall be revealed. He now by a kind of personification ascribes hope to them, as he did will before.

Romans 8:21: "Because the Creation itself," etc. He shows how the creation has in hope been made subject to vanity; that is, inasmuch as it shall some time be made free, according to what Isaiah testifies, and what Peter confirms still more clearly. It is then indeed meet for us to consider what a dreadful curse we have deserved, since all created things in themselves blameless, both on earth and in the visible heaven, undergo punishment for our sins; for it has not happened through their own fault, that they are liable to corruption. Thus the condemnation of mankind is imprinted on the heavens, and on the earth, and on all creatures. It hence also appears to what excelling glory the sons of God shall be exalted; for all creatures shall be renewed in order to amplify it, and to render it illustrious.

But he means not that all creatures shall be partakers of the same glory with the sons of God; but that they, according to their nature, shall be participators of a better condition; for God will restore to a perfect state the world, now fallen, together with mankind. But what that perfection will be, as to beasts as well as plants and metals, it is not meet nor right in us to inquire more curiously; for the chief effect of corruption is decay. Some subtle men, but hardly soberminded, inquire whether all kinds of animals will be immortal; but if reins be give to speculations where will they at length lead us? Let us then be content with this simple doctrine—that such will be the constitution and the complete order of things, that nothing will be deformed or fading.

Romans 8:22: "For we know," etc. He repeats the same sentiment, that he might pass over to us, though what is now said has the effect and the form of a conclusion; for as creatures are subject to corruption, not through their natural desire, but through the appointment of God, and then, as they have a hope of being hereafter freed from corruption, it hence follows, that they groan like a woman in travail until they shall be delivered. But it is a most suitable similitude; it shows that the groaning of which he speaks will not be in vain and without effect; for it will at length bring forth a joyful and blessed fruit. The meaning is, that creatures are not content in their present state, and yet that they are not so distressed that they pine away without a prospect of a remedy, but that they are as it were in travail; for a restoration of a better state awaits them. By saying that they groan together, he does not mean that they are united together by mutual anxiety, but he joins them as companions to us. The particle (hitherto), or, to this day, serves to alleviate the weariness of daily languor; for if creatures have continued for so many ages in their groaning, how inexcusable will our softness or sloth be if we faint during the short course of a shadowy life.

The Life of John Calvin

John Calvin was a Frenchman born in 1509 in Noyon, Picardy, about sixty miles from Paris. He was the youngest of four or possibly five children. All were boys. His mother, the daughter of a town notable, died four years after Calvin's birth, and after his father remarried he was sent from his father's house to live with a neighboring noble family. There he received some of his earliest education. Calvin and his father never did have a good relationship, partly because his father was fifty when he was born and his mother had died when he was so young. His siblings did not pursue intellectual studies, as did John, thus a close family bond did not exist.

John Calvin was from an early age very ambitious. When he was twelve his father sent him to the University of Paris to be a priest. Calvin there became attracted to evangelical humanism and its energizing spirituality. His father decided later that John should become a lawyer with its monetary benefits. Calvin obeyed, getting his degree in law, but was still fascinated with his humanistic studies. His father died shortly after and John was free to pursue his goals.

He was a writer of great works, but even though his theological dissertation was of value, he did not truly commit himself to salvation for some time and it was a conscious submission of his will to that of God on a more intellectual level. Though he became one of the leading reformers of the Protestant church he was never ordained in the Catholic Church as his father had initially wanted, or in a Protestant ministry. He was an excellent scholar, preacher and teacher of the Bible. He wanted to write and enjoyed those of the philosophical and religious circles. The college, College de France, had a humanistic approach to learning, which most suited his personality. At that time he embraced the philosophy of Erasmus. He was also very drawn to Aristotle and his teachings, which influenced him no doubt on his perception concerning women and animals as well believing that women were less intelligent and more prone to gossip than men.

Calvin was not interested in marriage though his friend Bucer advised him to marry and selected a lady for him; but Calvin rejected her. He did marry a widow with two children from a previous marriage. They were married in August 1540 and had at least three children, but all died in infancy. Though Calvin did not seek to marry for love, but more in order to have his home kept (a marriage of convenience, one might say), the marriage was a very good one and when his wife died only nine years later, he spoke of much pain and sorrow in his loss. Calvin was one who did not appear to feel great emotion even when his children died. He felt it his duty to refrain from any outward emotion of grief. He never remarried but assured his wife that he would care for her two children.

He was always torn between two philosophies of living. One was as a stoic, strong, intellectual, rational man and the other was one of pleasing others and embracing new, unexplored ideas in his Christian growth.

Calvin had a great fear of death and judgment. He felt that anxiety was not a good example consistent with his faith yet he had anxiety about many things, which attributed to his early death. No doubt some of his fear came from growing up without a secure and loving home life. With a demanding father he felt the only way to survive was to strive for perfection in his studies, and in pleasing those who could help and enable him to achieve success; and added to that was his strict attitude toward being obedient to God. He was truly a man of God but he put so many restrictions upon himself trying to live a righteous life, and was so outspoken on issues such as his attitude toward women, various Christian doctrines, and could not stand unkempt, unclean people, along with other intolerances that created much stress. This possibly helped bring about numerous diseases such as arthritis, inflammation of the kidneys, intestinal problems, bleeding from the stomach, hemorrhoids, and gout, a disease that causes inflammation of the joints, and led to his death in 1564.

Calvin was not only strict in his own personal life but in demanding that of his congregation as well. Calvin became the most outspoken and driven of all of the Protestant reformers of the time and found a base in Geneva, Switzerland. His doctrine, though Protestant, varied from Luther, whom he did most admire in several ways. He contributed the revelation of salvation by Grace, which Luther espoused, but his view differed from Luther's in that the doctrine of Luther states that man has a free will to choose salvation through Jesus Christ. Calvin believed that though man has a free will, he is predestined by God to either go to heaven or hell, as he believed God has decreed those who would go to heaven and those who would not before they were born. In Catholic dogma, salvation was offered to all men; none were excluded from it. The doctrine of John Wesley and the Methodist church agreed with Luther and the Roman Catholic Church.

Though Calvin liked music he did away with all instrumental music. The congregation did, however, sing psalms, which ministered to their hearts just as today, and was a great form of worship.

He believed that one controlled their own goodness on earth and any dependence or strength came from ones own inner convictions not that of anyone else. Calvin believed that man was sinful and could approach God only through faith in Christ, as did the other Protestant reformers. Good works were consequences of union with Christ in faith, not the means of salvation. Calvin laid down a set of laws, which governed the people morally and spiritually. Calvin did not believe in a hierarchy in the church.

Calvin preached on the average of 170 sermons a year, totaling over 4,000 in his lifetime.

CHAPTER 12

John Wesley and "The General Deliverance of Creation"

References:

- *The Journal of the Rev. John Wesley, A.M,* Bicentenary Issue, 1938, Volume IV
- *The Journal of the Rev. John Wesley, A.M.* Bicentenary Issue, 1938, Volume VIII
- *The Journal of John Wesley,* edited by Percy Livingstone Parker, with Introduction by Hugh Price Hughes, M.A. and "An Appreciation of John Wesley's Journal" by Augustine Birell, K.C.
- *John Wesley* works London 1860 vi Sermon LVI, *God's approbation of His works* 12860 vi Sermon LX Ser. 2, *"The General Deliverance"* Sec.III Par.9, *John Wesley Journals,* 1742; *"General Deliverance"* text from the 1872 edition

John Wesley was the founder of the Methodist church. Wesley was the most charismatic and far-reaching of all the early Protestant reformers. Within his sermons on the word of God he includes "The General Deliverance" sermon, which includes all creation.

"The General Deliverance" (Text from the 1872 edition)

SERMON SIXTY THE GENERAL DELIVERANCE: *"The earnest expectation of the creature waiteth for the manifestation of the sons of God. For the creature was made subject to vanity, not willingly, but by reason of him that subjected it: Yet in hope that the creature itself also shall be delivered from the bondage of corruption, into the glorious liberty of the sons of God. For we know that the whole creation groaneth, and travaileth in pain together until now."* (Romans 8:19-22)

1. Nothing is surer, than that as "the Lord is loving to every man, so "his mercy is over all his works;" all that have sense all that are capable of pleasure or pain, of happiness or misery. In consequence of this, "He openeth his hand, and filleth all things living with plenteousness. He prepareth food for cattle," as well as "herbs for the children of men." He provideth for the fowls of the air, "feeding the young ravens when they cry unto him." "He sendeth the springs into the rivers, that run among the hills, to give drink to every beast of the field," and that even "the wild asses may quench their thirst." And, suitably to this, he directs us to be tender of even the meaner creatures; to show mercy to these also. "Thou shalt not muzzle the ox that treadeth out the corn"—a custom which is observed in the eastern countries even to this day. And this is by no means contradicted by St. Paul's question: "Doth God take care for oxen?" Without doubt he does. We cannot deny it, without flatly contradicting his word. The plain meaning of the Apostle is, this all that is implied in the text? Hath it not a farther meaning? Does it not teach us, we are to feed the bodies of those whom we desire to feed our souls? Meantime it is certain; God "giveth grass for the cattle," as well as "herbs for the use of men."

2. But how are these Scriptures reconcilable to the present state of things? How are they consistent with what we daily see round about us, in every part of the creation? If the Creator and Father of every living thing is rich in mercy towards all; if he does not overlook or despise any of the works of his own hands; if he wills even the meanest of them to be happy, according to their degree; how comes it to pass, that such a complication of evils oppresses, yea, overwhelms them? How is it that misery of all kinds overspreads the face of the earth? This is a question which has puzzled the wisest philosophers in all ages: And it cannot be answered without having recourse to the oracles of God. But, taking these for our guide we may inquire,

I. What was the original state of the brute creation?

II. In what state is it at present? And,

III. In what state will it be at the manifestation of the children of God?

I. What was the original state of brute creation?

1. We may inquire, in the first place, what was the original state of the brute creation? And may we not learn this, even from the place which was assigned them; namely, the garden of God? All the beasts of the field, and all the fowls of the air, were with Adam in paradise. And there is no question but their state was suited to their place: It was paradisiacal; perfectly happy. Undoubtedly it bore a near resemblance to the state of man himself. By taking, therefore, a short view of the one (man), we may conceive the other (non-human creation). Now, "man was made in the image of God." But "God is a Spirit:" So therefore was man. (Only that spirit, being designed to dwell on earth, was lodged in an earthly tabernacle.) As such, he had an innate principle of self-motion. And so, it seems, has every spirit in the universe; this being the proper distinguishing difference between spirit and matter, which is totally, essentially passive and inactive, as appears from a thousand experiments. He was, after the likeness of his Creator, gifted with understanding (much more than animals), a capacity of apprehending whatever objects were brought before him, and of judging concerning them. He was gifted or given a will, using it in various affections and passions: And, lastly, with liberty, or freedom of choice (in other words a free will to chose what he wanted to chose, good, bad, etc). Without this free will all the rest would have been in vain, and he would have been no more capable of serving his Creator than a piece of earth or marble. He would have been as incapable of vice or virtue, as any part of the inanimate creation. In these, in the power of self-motion, understanding, will, and liberty, the natural image of God consisted.

[Wesley is speaking here of the free will God gave man alone to choose to follow Him or Satan and make this highest form of decisions, even to the extent of the destruction of others' lives. Animals do have a will to make decisions but God did not give them the free will to choose or distinguish (in most cases) good or evil. The non-human creation was put under the dominion of man who was to rule over them in kindness and love, protecting them and providing for those chosen to be of service to man. And therefore whatever decision man made directly affected the fate of the animal world. — MBP]

2. How far man's power of self-motion then extended; it is impossible for us to determine (before man sinned). It is probable, that he had a far higher degree both of swiftness and strength, than any of his descendants ever had, and much less any of the lower creatures. It is certain; he had such strength of understanding as no man ever since had. His understanding was perfect in its kind; capable of apprehending all things clearly, and judging concerning them according to truth, without any mixture of error. His will had no wrong bias of any sort; but all his passions and affections were regular, (normal which was perfect before sin) guided by his unmistakable understanding; embracing nothing but good. His liberty likewise was wholly guided by his understanding: He chose, or refused, according to its direction. Above all, (which was man's highest excellence, far more valuable than all the rest put together,) he was a creature capable of God; capable of knowing, loving, and obeying his Creator. And, in fact, he did know God, did sincerely love and uniformly obey him. This was the supreme perfection of man; (as it is of all intelligent beings) the continually seeing, and loving, and obeying the Father of the spirits of all flesh. From this right state and right use of all his faculties, his happiness naturally flowed. In this the essence of his happiness consisted; but it was increased by all the things that were round about him. He saw, with unspeakable pleasure, the order, the beauty, the harmony, of all the creatures; of all animated, all inanimate nature; the serenity of the

skies; the sun walking in brightness; the sweetly varied colors of the earth; the trees, the fruits, the flowers, and splashing sounds of murmuring streams. Nor was this pleasure interrupted by evil of any kind. It had no mixture of sorrow or pain, whether of body or mind. For while man was innocent he was impassive; incapable of suffering. Nothing could stain his purity of joy. And, to crown all, he was immortal.

3. To this creature, man, gifted with all these excellent faculties, thus qualified for his high charge, God said, *"Have thou dominion over the fish of the sea, and over the fowl of the air, and over every living thing that moveth upon the earth."* (Gen. 1:28.) And so the Psalmist: *"Thou madest him to have dominion over the works of thy hands: Thou hast put all things under his feet: All sheep and oxen, yea, and the beasts of the field, the fowl of the air, and the fish of the sea, and whatsoever passeth through the paths of the seas."* (Psalm 8:6 etc.) So that man was God's deputy regent, the prince and governor of this lower world; and all the blessings of God flowed through him to the inferior creatures. Man was the channel of conveyance between his Creator and the whole brute creation.

4. But what blessings were those that were then conveyed through man to the lower creatures? What was the original state of the brute creatures, when they were first created? This deserves a more attentive consideration than has been usually given it. It is certain these, as well as man, had an innate principle of self-motion; and that, at least, in as high a degree as they enjoy it at this day. Again: They were endued with a degree of understanding; not less than that they are possessed of now. They had also a will, including various passions, which, likewise, they still enjoy: And they had liberty, a power of choice; a degree of which is still found in every living creature. Nor can we doubt but their understanding too was, in the beginning, perfect in its kind. Their passions and affections were regular, and their choice always guided by their understanding

5. What then is the barrier between men and brutes? The line

which they cannot pass? It was not reason. Set aside that ambiguous term: Exchange it for the plain word, understanding: and who can deny that brutes have this? We may as well deny that they have sight or hearing. But it is this: Man is capable of God; the inferior creatures are not. We have no ground to believe that they are, in any degree, capable of knowing, loving, or obeying God. This is the specific difference between man and brute; the great gulf which they cannot pass over. And as a loving obedience to God was the perfection of man, so a loving obedience to man was the perfection of brutes. And as long as they continued in this, they were happy after their kind; happy in the right state and the right use of their respective faculties. Yea, and so long they had some shadowy resemblance of even moral goodness. For they had gratitude to man for benefits received, and a reverence for him. They had likewise a kind of benevolence to each other, unmixed with any contrary temper. How beautiful many of them were, we may conclude from that which still remains; and that not only in the noblest creatures, but in those of the lowest order. And they were all surrounded, not only with plenteous food, but with every thing that could give them pleasure; pleasure unmixed with pain; for pain was not yet; it had not entered into paradise. And they too were immortal: For "God made not death; neither hath he pleasure in the death of any living."

[John Wesley stated that there are no grounds for believing that animals are capable of knowing, loving or obeying God; however, Scriptures tell us they do know, obey and praise God. I do not hold this against Wesley. He fully understands they do go to heaven and why they fell into corruption, and that they are to be treated humanely. I have to rely on Scripture and thus according to such have learned that animals praise God. In many cases they are obedient to Him according to many scriptures, and in praising Him, they would have to love Him to want to praise Him. And it is possible in their own way they have a form of prayer to God because they know to praise Him so would they not be capable of prayers which is in a way a form of praise. Even in our limited earthly understanding and observation, we know animals are capable of love, some very, very deep love and certainly are taught to obey. And what is true on earth is true in heaven. Their innocence keeps them spiritually connected with their Creator. — MBP]

6. How true then is that word, "God saw everything that he had made: and behold it was very good!" But how far is this from being the present case! In what a condition is the whole lower world! To say nothing of inanimate nature, wherein all the elements seem to be out of course, and fight against man. Since man rebelled against his Maker, in what a state is all animated nature! Well might the Apostle say of this: *"The whole creation groaneth and travaileth together in pain until now."* This directly refers to the brute creation in what state this is at present we are now to consider.

II. In what stage is it at present?

1. As all the blessings of God in paradise flowed through man to the inferior creatures; as man was the great channel of communication, between the Creator and the whole brute creation; so when man made himself incapable of transmitting those blessings, that communication was necessarily cut off. [In a true sense here it is: the blessings of perfection, just as man, the animals now get disease; God does not walk among us. Man has to go through Christ in this time for healing and for pleading healing for the animals. etc. — MBP] The intercourse between God and the inferior creatures being stopped, those blessings could no longer flow in upon them. And then it was that "the creature," every creature, "was subjected to vanity," to sorrow, to pain of every kind, to all manner of evils: Not, indeed, "willingly," not by its own choice, not by any act or deed of its own; "but by reason of Him that subjected it," by the wise permission of God, determining to draw eternal good out of this temporary evil.

2. But in what respect was "the creature," every creature, then "made subject to vanity?" (Vanity means uselessness, worthlessness,

lack of value.) What did the meaner creatures suffer, when man rebelled against God? It is probable they sustained much loss, even in the lower faculties: their vigor, strength, and swiftness. But undoubtedly they suffered far more in their (intelligence) understanding; more than we can easily conceive. Perhaps insects and worms had then as much understanding as the most intelligent brutes have now: Whereas millions of creatures have, at present, little more understanding than the earth on which they crawl, or the rock to which they adhere. They suffered still more in their will, in their passions; which were then variously distorted, and frequently set in flat opposition to the little understanding that was left them. Their liberty, likewise, was greatly impaired; yea, in many cases, totally destroyed. They are still utterly enslaved to irrational appetites, which have the full dominion over them. The very foundations of their nature are out of course; are turned upside down. As man is deprived of *his* perfection, his loving obedience to God; so brutes are deprived of *their* perfection, their loving obedience to man. The far greater part of them flee from him; studiously avoid his hated presence. The most of the rest set him at open defiance; yea, destroy him, if it be in their power. A few only, those we commonly term domestic animals, retain more or less of their original disposition, through the mercy of God, love him still, and pay obedience to him.

3. Setting these few aside, how little shadow of good, of gratitude, of benevolence, of any right temper, is now to be found in any part of the brute creation! On the contrary, what savage fierceness, what unrelenting cruelty; are constantly observed in thousands of creatures; is inseparable from their natures! Is it only the lion, the tiger, the wolf, among the inhabitants of the forest and plains, the shark, and a few more voracious monsters, among the inhabitants of the waters, or the eagle, among birds, that tears the flesh, sucks the blood, and crushes the bones of their helpless fellow-creatures? Nay; the harmless fly, the laborious ant, the painted butterfly, are treated in the same merciless manner, even by the innocent songsters of the

grove! The innumerable tribes of poor insects are continually devoured by them. And whereas there is but a small number, comparatively, of beasts of prey on the earth, it is quite otherwise in the liquid element. There are but few inhabitants of the waters, whether of the sea, or of the rivers, which do not devour whatsoever they can master: Yea, they exceed herein all the beasts of the forest, and all the birds of prey. For none of these have been ever observed to prey upon their own species:

Even savage bears will not each other tear. But the water-savages swallow up all, even of their own kind, that are smaller and weaker than themselves. Yes, such, at present, is the miserable constitution of the world, to such vanity is it now subjected, that an immense majority of creatures, perhaps a million to one, can no otherwise preserve their own lives, than by destroying their fellow-creatures!

4. And is not the very form, the outward appearance, of many of the creatures, as horrid as their dispositions? Where is the beauty which was stamped upon them when they came first out of the hands of their Creator? There is not the least trace of it left: So far from it, that they are shocking to behold! Nay, they are not only terrible and grisly to look upon, but deformed, and that to a high degree. Yet their features, ugly as they are at best, are frequently made more deformed than usual, when they are distorted by pain; which they cannot avoid, any more than the wretched sons of men. Pain of various kinds, weakness, sickness, and diseases innumerable, come upon them; perhaps from within; perhaps from one another; perhaps from the inclemency of seasons; from fire, hail, snow, or storm; or from a thousand causes which they cannot foresee or prevent.

5. Thus, "as by one man sin entered into the world, and death by sin; even so death passed upon all men"; and not on man only, but on those creatures also that "did not sin after the similitude of Adam's transgression." And not death alone came upon them, but all of its train of preparatory evils; pain, and ten thousand sufferings. Nor these only, but likewise all those irregular passions, all those

unlovely tempers (which in men are sins, and even in the brutes are sources of misery), "passed upon all" the inhabitants of the earth; and remain in all, except the children of God.

6. During this season of vanity, not only the feebler creatures are continually destroyed by the stronger; not only the strong are frequently destroyed by those that are of equal strength; but both the one and the other are exposed to the violence and cruelty of him that is now their common enemy—man. And if his swiftness or strength is not equal to theirs, yet his art more than supplies that defect. By this he avoids all their force, how great so ever it be; by this he defeats all their swiftness; and, notwithstanding their various shifts and schemes, discovers all their retreats. He pursues them over the widest plains, and through the thickest forests. He overtakes them in the fields of air; he finds them out in the depths of the sea. Nor are the mild and friendly creatures that still know his moves, and are obedient to his commands, secured thereby from more than brutal violence; from outrage and abuse of various kinds. Is the generous horse that serves his master's necessity or pleasure with unwearied diligence; is the faithful dog that waits the motion of his hand, or his eye, exempt from this? What returns for their long and faithful service do many of these poor creatures find? And what a dreadful difference is there, between what they suffer from their fellow-brutes, and what they suffer from the tyrant man! The lion, the tiger, or the shark, gives them pain from mere necessity, in order to prolong their own life; and put them out of their pain at once: But the human shark, without any such necessity, torments them of his free choice; and perhaps continues their lingering pain till, after months or years, death signs their release.

III. In what state will it be at the manifestation of the children of God?

1. But will "the creature," will even the brute creation, always remain in this deplorable condition? God forbid that we should affirm this; yea or even entertain such a thought! While "the whole

creation groaneth together" (whether men attend or not), their groans are not dispersed in idle air, but enter into the ears of Him that made them. While his creatures "travail together in pain," he knoweth all their pain, and is bringing them nearer and nearer to the birth, which shall be accomplished in its season. He seeth "the earnest expectation" wherewith the whole animated creation "waiteth for" that final "manifestation of the sons of God;" in which "they themselves also shall be delivered" (not by annihilation; annihilation is not deliverance) from the present "bondage of corruption," into a measure of "the glorious liberty of the children of God."

2. Nothing can be more express: Away with vulgar prejudices, and let the plain word of God take place. They "shall be delivered from the bondage of corruption, into glorious liberty"—even a measure, according as they are capable—of "the liberty of the children of God."

A general view of this is given us in the twenty-first chapter of the Revelation. When He that "sitteth on the great white throne" hath pronounced, "Behold, I make all things new" when the word is fulfilled, "The tabernacle of God is with men, and they shall be his people, and God himself shall be with them and be their God"— then the following blessing shall take place (not only on the children of men; there is no such restriction in the text; but) on every creature according to its capacity: "God shall wipe away all tears from their eyes. And there shall be no more death, neither sorrow, nor crying. Neither shall there be any more pain: For the former things are passed away."

3. To descend to a few particulars: The whole brute creation will then, undoubtedly, be restored, not only to the vigor, strength, and swiftness which they had at their creation, but to a far higher degree of each than they ever enjoyed. They will be restored, not only to that measure of understanding which they had in paradise, but to a degree of it as much higher than that, as the understanding of an elephant is beyond that of a worm. And whatever affections they had

in the garden of God, will be restored with vast increase; being exalted and refined in a manner which we ourselves are not now able to comprehend. The liberty they then had will be completely restored, and they will be free in all their motions. They will be delivered from all irregular appetites, from all unruly passions, from every disposition that is either evil in itself, or has any tendency to evil. No rage will be found in any creature, no fierceness, no cruelty, or thirst for blood. So far from it that "the wolf shall dwell with the lamb, the leopard shall lie down with the kid; the calf and the young lion together; and a little child shall lead them. The cow and the bear shall feed together; and the lion shall eat straw like the ox. They shall not hurt nor destroy in all my holy mountain." (Isaiah 11:6 etc.)

4. Thus, in that day, all the vanity to which they are now helplessly subject will be abolished; they will suffer no more, either from within or without; the days of their groaning are ended. At the same time, there can be no reasonable doubt, but all the horridness of their appearance, and all the deformity of their aspect, will vanish away, and be exchanged for their primeval beauty. And with their beauty their happiness will return; to which there can then be no obstruction. As there will be nothing within, so there will be nothing without, to give them any uneasiness: No heat or cold, no storm or tempest, but one perennial spring. In the new earth, as well as in the new heavens, there will be nothing to give pain, but everything that the wisdom and goodness of God can create to give happiness. As a recompense for what they once suffered, while under the "bondage of corruption," when God has "renewed the face of the earth," and their corruptible body has put on incorruption, they shall enjoy happiness suited to their state, without alloy, without interruption, and without end.

5. But though I doubt not that the Father of All has a tender regard for even his lowest creatures, and that, in consequence of this, he will make them large amends for all they suffer while under their present bondage; yet I dare not affirm that he has an *equal regard* for

them and for the children of men. I do not believe that He sees *with equal eyes*, as Lord of all, a hero perish, or a sparrow fall. By no means. This is exceeding pretty; but it is absolutely false. For though Mercy, with truth and endless grace, o'er all his works doth reign, yet chiefly he delights to bless His favorite creature, man.

God regards his meanest creatures much; but he regards man much more. He does not *equally* regard a hero and a sparrow; the best of men and the lowest of brutes. "How *much more* does your heavenly Father care for you!" says He "who is in the bosom of his Father." Those who thus strain the point are clearly confuted by his question, "Are not ye *much better* than they?" Let it suffice, that God regards everything that he hath made, in its own order, and in proportion to that measure of his own image which he has stamped upon it.

6. May I be permitted to mention here a conjecture concerning the brute creation? What, if it should then please the all-wise, the all-gracious Creator to raise them higher in the scale of beings? What, if it should please him, when he makes us "equal to angels," to make them what we are now—creatures capable of God; capable of knowing and loving and enjoying the Author of their being? If it should be so, ought our eye to be evil because he is good? However this be, he will certainly do what will be most for his own glory.

7. If it be objected to all this (as very probably it will), "But of what use will those creatures be in that future state?" I answer this by another question, what use are they of now? If there be (as has commonly been supposed) eight thousand species of insects, who is able to inform us of what use seven thousand of them are? If there be four hundred sorts of beasts, to what use do three hundred of them serve? Consider this; consider how little we know of even the present designs of God; and then you will not wonder that we know still less of what he designs to do in the new heavens and the new earth.

8. "But what end does it answer to dwell upon this subject, which we so imperfectly understand?" To consider so much as we do

understand, so much as God has been pleased to reveal to us, may answer that excellent end—to illustrate that mercy of God which "is over all his works." And it may exceedingly confirm our belief that, much more; he is loving to every man... If "the Lord will save," as the inspired writer affirms, "both man and beast," in their several degrees, surely "the children of men may put their trust under the shadow of his wings!"

9. May it not answer another end; namely, furnish us with a full answer to a plausible objection against the justice of God, in suffering numberless creatures that never had sinned to be so severely punished? They could not sin, for they were not moral agents. Yet how severely do they suffer! Yea, many of them, beasts of burden in particular, almost the whole time of their abode on earth; so that they can have no retribution here below. But the objection vanishes away, if we consider that something better remains after death for these poor creatures also; that these, likewise, shall one day be delivered from this bondage of corruption, and shall then receive an ample amends for all their present sufferings.

10. One more excellent end may undoubtedly be answered by the preceding considerations. They may encourage us to imitate Him whose mercy is over all his works. They may soften our hearts towards the meaner creatures, knowing that the Lord careth for them. It may enlarge our hearts towards those poor creatures, to reflect that, as vile as they appear in our eyes, not one of them is forgotten in the sight of our Father which is in heaven. Through all the vanity to which they are now subjected, let us look to what God hath prepared for them. Yea, let us habituate ourselves to look forward, beyond this present scene of bondage, to the happy time when they will be delivered from there into the liberty of the children of God.

11. From what has been said, I cannot but draw one inference, which no man of reason can deny. If it is this which distinguishes men from beasts—that they are creatures capable of God, capable of knowing and loving and enjoying him; then whoever is "without

God in the world," whoever does not know or love or enjoy God and is not careful about the matter, does, in effect, disclaim the nature of man, and degrade himself into a beast. Let such vouchsafe a little attention to those remarkable words of Solomon: "I said in my heart concerning the estate of the sons of men, they might see that they themselves are beasts." (Eccles. 3:18.) These sons of men are undoubtedly beasts; and that by their own act and deed; for they deliberately and willfully disclaim the sole characteristic of human nature. It is true, they may have a share of reason; they have speech, and they walk erect; but they have not the mark, the only mark, which totally separates man from the brute creation. "That which befalleth beasts, the same thing befalleth them." They are equally without God in the world; "so that a man" of this kind "hath no preeminence above a beast."

12. So much more let all those who are of a nobler turn of mind assert the distinguishing dignity of their nature. Let all those who are of a more generous spirit know and maintain their rank in the scale of beings. Rest not till you enjoy the privilege of humanity—the knowledge and love of God. Lift your heads, ye creatures capable of God! Lift up your hearts to the Source of your being! Know God, and teach your souls to know the joys that from religion flow. Give your hearts to Him who, together with ten thousand blessings, has given you his Son, his only Son! Let your continual "fellowship be with the Father, and with his Son, Jesus Christ!" Let God be in all your thoughts and ye will be men indeed. Let him be your God and your all—the desire of your eyes, the joy of your heart, and your portion for ever.

The Life of John Wesley

The greatest compliment possibly given to John Wesley was from Bishop Asbury in his *Journal:* "When we consider his plain and nervous writings, his uncommon talent for sermonizing and journalizing ...his knowledge as an observer; his attainments as a scholar; his experience as a Christian; I conclude his equal is not to be found among all the sons he hath brought up, nor his superior among all the sons of Adam he may have left behind."

During the eighteenth, nineteenth, and twentieth centuries, no other man has influenced the spread of Christianity more than John Wesley. John Wesley and his colleagues were the first preachers since the days of the Franciscan Friars in the Middle Ages who reached the working classes. The Reformation was basically the middle-class movement in England, France and Germany. It never reached the upper class or the working class.

Augustine Birrell states that Wesley was himself "the greatest force of the eighteenth century in England. No single figure influenced so many minds; no single voice touched so many hearts. No other man did such a life's work for England." Wesley had demonstrated that a true prophet of God has more influence than all the politicians do and soldiers and millionaires put together. He is the incalculable and unexpected element that is always putting all the devices of the clever to naught.

John Wesley was born in 1703 in Epworth in Lincolnshire, England. In 1714 he was admitted to Charterhouse School in London and in 1720 was an undergraduate at Christ Church, Oxford. Wesley was ordained a deacon in 1725, and Elected Fellow of Lincoln College at Oxford in 1726. He passed away on March 3, 1791, at City Road in London, at age 88. He preached for the better part of the eighteenth century, not stopping until just before his death. He started his outdoor preaching in 1739 after the example of his fellow minister, Rev. Whitefield.

He was rescued from his father's rectory at Epworth, England, by a neighbor when he was six. He strongly believed God saved him for a special mission. John Wesley's great-grandfather and grandfather were ministers, yet were harassed and suffered from the hands of others due to their conservatism, which marked the family for generations. His great-grandfather and grandfather were ejected from their livings and the grandfather was even refused a Christian burial, though he was a most holy and God-fearing man.

John was schooled in a classical setting at Charterhouse and Christ Church. He was at home in the best of company due to his intelligence, moral constitution, and willingness to reach out to the needs of the world. He fought to make sure that even those in prison were clothed properly, had blankets to keep them warm and enough food to eat. John Wesley would be become the spiritual advocate for the working class of Europe.

John Wesley compiled his first collection of hymns, *The Charleston Hymnal,* in 1737. Many songs from the Methodist hymnal are sung in Christian churches today.

He and his brother Charles sailed to America in 1737 to preach to the American Indians, slaves and other colonists, but this experience was not a happy one for him. Finally, after much conflict concerning a Miss Sophy Hopkey, whom he had courted and with whom he seemed hesitant to marry until it was too late (she, apparently feeling the relationship hopeless, married in haste a Mr. Williamson), he had little option other than to return to England due to some slightly unacceptable religious accusations aimed at her, thus refusing her communion. This was a serious judgment on his part and Sophy and her husband sought correction to the matter by insisting Wesley apologize and give Sophy communion. Most of the people of the church backed Sophy; thus Wesley found himself in a very unacceptable position. As a result he left America to return to England.

The experience was to be a blessing in disguise, as upon his return he attended a Moravian meeting (a Christian denomination descended from the Bohemian Brethren) in which he became completely converted to Christ. Wesley states he felt his heart "strangely warmed" while the Epistle to the Romans was being read. A similar experience had come to his younger brother Charles just three days before and to his fellow preacher Whitefield a little earlier.

John Wesley married Mary Vazeille, a widow who had a daughter, in 1751. Their marriage was not a happy one and she eventually left him in 1758, although he remained true to their marriage vows.

His main form of transportation was horseback. He created a group of ministers known as the "circuit riders." In America, the ministers went by horseback from town to town to preach the gospel. He himself traveled around eight thousand miles each year and seldom preached less than one thousand times each year during his fifty-plus years in the ministry. He boldly preached the Gospel to whoever would hear him. He never knew what it was to be depressed of spirit, yet he was spit at, cursed continuously, accused of preaching false doctrine, run out of towns, had bulls let out to chase him down, had numerous stones and mud slung at him, had a jealous wife, and suits in chancery (accused of preaching false doctrine). He rode in terribly cold and snowy weather and in rain and the heat of summer, yet his disposition remained totally upbeat, never giving up on his cause to spread the love of Jesus throughout Europe and to tell all who would hear that the only way to heaven was redemption through the blood of Jesus. With so many adversaries, one of Wesley's great virtues was his ability to forgive all malice from the cruelest enemy. He looked and believed in the best of others, even though he was often quite disappointed.

He was a very charismatic and exciting preacher, yet quiet in manner. He was slender and nice looking, not tall in stature but he was meticulous in dress and organization. He did not like being around negative and ill-tempered people.

Wesley also learned that one could be miraculously healed, as well as one's horse. He praised God for that blessing. Concerning healing of man and beast he wrote: "My horse was very lame, yet I rode seven miles having a bad headache. Then it occurred to me to ask God for healing and (What I here state is the naked fact: let every man account for it as he sees good.) I then thought, 'Cannot God heal either man or beast, by any means, or without any?' Immediately my weariness and headache ceased, and my horse's lameness in the same instant. Nor did he halt any more either that day or the next. A very odd accident this also!"

Wesley had numerous remedies besides prayer for curing the sick. One of the remedies was applying brier leaf to stop violent bleeding. He also used electric shock for cures of various illnesses and or disorders. He electrified several who were ill of various disorders. Some were immediately cured and some gradually. Wesley also used herbs for various illnesses. He was a kind of amateur doctor. He also felt strongly about the abilities of the medical doctors. Wesley spoke out on doctors of his time who could not diagnose causes of much pain and suffering, as in the case of a poor woman who had lost her son and was suffering from severe pain in the stomach over the grief of losing her dear little one. Wesley stated: "They prescribe drug upon drug, without knowing a jot of the matter concerning the root of the disorder. And without knowing this they cannot cure, though they can murder the patient. Whence came this woman's pain (which she would never had told had she never been questioned about it), fretting for the death of her son. And what availed medicines while that fretting continued. Why, then, do not all physicians consider how far bodily disorders are caused or influenced by the mind and in those cases which are utterly out of their sphere call in the assistance of a minister, as ministers, when they find the mind disordered by the body, call in the assistance of a physician? But why are these cases out of their sphere? Because they know not God. It follows; no man can be a thorough physician without being an experienced Christian."

Quite often people would fall out in the Spirit, as today we see people do in the more Pentecostal churches, while he and his fellow ministers were preaching.

Wesley experienced demon possession in others upon occasion. He would pray to rid the victim of demon possession until there was a breakthrough, and often this took hours. He witnessed those with contorted bodies, screaming, worshiping Satan in word and manner. At times there were more than one possessed and his fellow ministers would stand praying until the demons had left the person and the person was praising God and exhausted, joyful to be rid of such horrors and anguish. And though Wesley truly believed in the various manifestations of the spirit and demon control he also knew that Satan could mimic and counterfeit God, so he warned others to seek God for divine revelation in such matters.

While preaching one morning to all very serious persons, an ass walked gravely in at the gate, came up to the door of the house, lifted up his head, and stood stock-still, in a posture of deep attention. Wesley remarked, "Might not the dumb beast reprove many who have far less decency and not much more understanding?"

Wesley had discovered a lion that was fond of music and that birds would sing when he sang and spoke of the word of God. Wesley spoke of a sermon he preached at a farmer's house near Brough. The sun was hot but some shady trees covered both Wesley and most of the congregation. There was one more guest to participate in the ministry, however: a little bird that perched on a limb, which sang without intermission from the beginning of the service unto the end.

Another time while preaching at eleven in the evening at Coolylough, the congregation was singing, and to their surprise, all of the horses from all parts of the ground gathered about them. Wesley determined that horses, as well as lions and tigers, have an ear for music.

Augustine Birrell stated: "No man lived nearer the center than John Wesley. You cannot cut him out of our national life. No single figure influenced so many minds; no single voice touched so many hearts. No other man did such a life's work for England. John Wesley was ever a preacher and an organizer. John Wesley kept the Gospel of salvation and the doctrine of the Methodist church alive and his organizational skills set it up in such a way that it flourished in England and in America."

Wesley had a full and productive life, preaching until just a few months before his death. His last hours ended with: "There is no way into the holiest but by the blood of Jesus."

CHAPTER 13

Jewish and Muslim
Tradition Concerning Animals

In him all things were created, in heaven and on earth...
all things were created through him and for him.
(Colossians 1:16 RSV)

References:
- Muhammad Pickthall, *The Glorious Quran*
- Al-Hafz B.A. Masri, statements from the Quran and *Muslim Viewpoint*

The Islamic Quran speaks of the fair treatment of animals and of man's chastisement concerning any cruelty they suffer at the hands of man. God told man after he fell that they would have to work for their food but He provided food for the animals. We are now in such competition with them, that animals have had to alter their diet in more ways than God had created them to eat. They were created to eat only vegetation, along with man. Many of the animal world do not eat anything but vegetation, but some God designed so that when man sinned and flesh started to decay on the earth there would be scavenger animals that would eat dead flesh and not get sick and to keep disease from spreading throughout the world. God also told man that we were to be caretakers of the animals and to treat them humanely and provide food for them, not letting them suffer unnecessarily.

The following text is taken from *The Glorious Quran*, Arabic Text and English Rendering by Muhammad Pickthall, and The Quran.

And there is not a beast in the earth but the sustenance thereof dependeth on Allah. He knoweth its habitation and its repository. All is in a clear record. (Quran, ch.11 v. 6)

And He it is Who sends the winds, glad tidings heralding his mercy; and We send down purifying water from the sky (49) That We may give life thereby to a dead land, and We give many beasts and men that We have created to drink thereof. (ch. 25, v. 48,49)

And the earth hath He appointed for (His) creatures. (ch. 55, v. 10)

Seeth thou not that it is Allah whose praises are celebrated by all beings in the heavens and on earth, and by the birds with extended wings? Each one knows its own [mode of] prayer and psalm. And Allah is aware of what they do. (ch. 24, v. 41)

The Quran states: *And your Lord revealed to the bee, saying: Make hives in the mountains, and in the trees, and in* [human] *habitations.* (ch. 16, v. 68)

And Solomon was David's heir, and he said: "O mankind! Lo! We have been taught the language of birds, and have been given (abundance) of all things. This surely is evident favour." (ch. 27, v. 16.)

And they were gathered together unto Solomon his armies of the jinn [any of a class of spirits, lower than angels, capable of appearing in human or animal form, and influencing mankind for good or evil] *and humankind, and of the birds, and they were set in battle order.* (ch. 27, v. 17)

Hast thou not seen that unto Allah payeth adoration whosoever is in the heavens and whosoever is in the earth, and the sun, and the moon, and the stars, and the hills, and the trees, and the beasts, and many of mankind, while there are many unto whom the doom is justly due. He whom Allah scorneth, there is none to give him honour. Lo! Allah doth what He will. (ch. 22 v. 18.)

Both the Islamic and Judaic religions have strict rules about the treatment of animals. They are to be killed only for food and other necessities and only by being stunned so they feel no pain before they are killed. Unfortunately neither religion follows those rules today.

Maulana Maududi, an honored Muslim theologian and founder of the Jama'at-i-Islami, stated: "God has honored man with authority over His countless creatures. This superior position does not mean that God has given him unbridled liberty."

The Quran speaks of some of the nations and how they fell into sin and perished. The Tribe of Samood were descendants of Noah. There was a prophet named Saleh who would speak of future happenings. The people of Samood demanded that the Prophet Saleh show them some sign to prove that he was a prophet of God. At that time the tribe was experiencing a lack of food and water and was, therefore, neglecting its livestock. It was revealed to the Prophet Saleh to single out a she-camel as a symbol and ask his people to give her a fair share of water and fodder. The people of Samood promised to do that, but later killed the camel. As retribution, the tribe was annihilated. (ch. 11, v. 64; ch. 26, vv. 155, 156; ch. 54, vv. 27-31)

Allah cursed him [Satan], but he [Satan] said: "I will get hold of some of your men, And I will lead them [human beings] astray And I will excite in them vain desires; And I will incite them to cut off the ears of cattle; And most certainly I will bid them to alter the Nature Created by Allah." (ch. 4, vv. 118-119) He promiseth them and stirreth up desires in them, and Satan promiseth them only to beguile. (ch. 4v 120) For such, their habitation will be hell, and they will find no refuge there. (ch. 4, v. 121)

Islam says that all the creation has certain rights upon man. Animals should not be needlessly hunted for sport. No animal is to be tortured or its life prolonged in any painful way. Animals are not to be caged unless it is beneficial to their own life. Animals are not to be used for luxuries or for testing for superficial benefits of humankind. Animals are not to be trapped in harmful devices causing them injury and possibly leading to a painful and prolonged death. And animals are not to be bred in confined, unclean quarters.

We think animals so savage, yet our very own kind have lived in tribes that not only hunt but also are cannibalistic as well. How often we forget just how savage and animalistic we human beings can be. It is said that after Adam sinned he shrank from ten cubits tall to three cubits tall. As I was reading about the size of the angels in the Bible, and accounts of those who have said they have seen them, the angels are very tall—about eight to ten feet—but those who claim they have seen the demons, which are the fallen angels, say they are very small. Some are only a foot or so tall or even smaller than that. In the beginning, all animals apparently spoke as did the snake, and there was no darkness, no one had to work, and all lived in peace.

In finding evidence of the treatment of animals by the Jewish people we find that they were far more humane and got their teachings concerning the need to treat animals humanely from the Old Testament scriptures, yet they understood the need for the sacrifices of innocent animals to cover their sins, understanding the hopeless sinful nature and soul of man. *Thou hast given [man] dominion over the works of they hands; thou hast put all things under his feet, all sheep and oxen, and also the beasts of the field, the birds of the air and the fish of the sea.* (Psalm 8:6-8 The Holy Scriptures) The animals were and are dependent on man for their very existence. They are entrusted to man, who has to be kind and provide for them. The animals are God's creation and they have a closeness to God we do not understand. Man will be accountable for His treatment of them.

CHAPTER 14

Sin and Redemption As It Affects Both Man and Animals

References:

- Robert Eisenman and Michael Wise, *The Dead Sea Scrolls Uncovered*
- Richard Bauckham, *The Theology of the Book of Revelation*
- Andrew Linzey, *Animal Theology*
- Josephus' Discourse to the Greeks Concerning Hades
- Matthew Henry's *Commentary*

Great anxiety has God allotted, and a heavy yoke, to the sons of men; from the day one leaves his mother's womb to the day he returns to the mother of all the living, (in foot notes says: The earth from which man was taken) [Cf. Gen. 2, 7 (17); 3, 19f (18); Job 1,21 Ps. 138, 15 (702)] his thoughts, the fear in his heart, and his troubled forebodings till the day he dies, whether he sits on a lofty throne or grovels in dust and ashes, whether he bears a splendid crown or is wrapped in the coarsest of cloaks are of wrath and envy, trouble and dread, terror of death, fury and strife. Even when he lies on his bed to rest, his cares at night disturb his sleep. So short is his rest it seems like none, till in his dreams he struggles as he did by day, terrified by what his mind's eye sees, like a fugitive being pursued; as he reaches safety, he wakes up astonished that there is nothing to fear. So it is with all flesh, with man and with beast, but for sinners seven times more. Plague and bloodshed, wrath and the sword, plunder and ruin famine and death: for the wicked, these were created evil, and it is they who bring on destruction. All that is of earth returns to earth, and what is from above returns above. (Sirach 40:1-11 St. Joseph's Bible) The inspired writer in this passage separates man and animals from the sinners. Only unrepentant sinners need fear death.

Each day you must offer a bull as a sacrifice, so that sin may be forgiven. (Exodus 29:36 GNB) This refers to the seven days of sacrifice in ordaining Aaron and his sons as Priests.

In the Vatican II doctrine of the Roman Catholic Church it is stated that the entire world will be fulfilled in Christ. First, sin separated the world from God. He had to send his son to restore creation back to himself. That meant that fallen man had to be redeemed at one point as he was given the free will to choose God or Satan. Until Jesus came, the animals were the sin atonement for a future time when the Savior would come to restore repentant mankind back to God. Leviticus 16:5-28 tells us that each year the people were to bring two he-goats for their sin offering and one ram for their burnt offering to the temple. The priest would kill the ram for the burnt offering and its blood would be sprinkled on the mercy seat of the temple. Lots were then cast and one he-goat would be offered to the Lord as a sin offering; the other would be presented alive before the Lord as a scapegoat. The rite of atonement would be placed over it and it would then be released into the wilderness.

Many come to the conclusion that animals are worthless, as God required the Israelites to sacrifice them so often. If we are to believe that the blood of the animals and their sacrifice to cover the sins of man is of no real value, their lives completely useless and not worthy of eternal life, we need to consider two things. One is that man had no other way to be redeemed before Christ came as man was sinful and all were contaminated; but the animal's blood (breath/spirit) was pure and sinless. God had no other choice if He wanted to save man from hell other than to sacrifice the sinless for the sinful. It was only through their blood that man could be covered and delivered from sin before Christ came. Second, if the animals were as nothing to God in requiring their sacrifice, how does that reflect the life and value many perceive that God puts on Jesus? Is it that we see no value in the sacrifice of the animals and their earthly and eternal worth nor really understand the real sacrifice, suffering, and resurrection of Jesus to restore man back to God?

Often God became very upset with the people because they were sacrificing animals in vain. Their hearts were not right and they were breaking their vows to God. They were just going through the rituals set down by Moses and not really confessing their sins and changing their lives to worship God. One example, Psalms 50:7-15, says to "offer unto God the sacrifice of praise and thanksgiving, and keep thou vows to God, but not the blood of the animals as they already belong to Him." And in the New Testament we find that though the animals' sacrifices did cover man's sins, now there is one final sacrifice to restore man back to God and this sacrifice was a onetime sacrifice for now and for the future generations as well. At this point the sacrifice of animals became a sin rather than restoration of man to God. Jesus was sacrificed once and for all to redeem man and creation back to God. (cf. Hebrews 9:11-14)

The Bible compares the innocent lamb and Jesus. Repentant man references the innocent, spotless and blemish-free animals in the Bible. In presenting Christians as holy, spotless and blameless the same applies to animals as well. A wonderful analogy is Jesus being compared to a lamb, spotless and blameless/without blemish. *But with the precious blood of Christ, as of a lamb without blemish and without spot.* (I Peter 1:19 KJV)

And unto the children of Israel thou shalt speak, saying, Take ye a kid of the goats for a sin offering; and a calf and a lamb, both of the first year, without blemish, for a burnt offering. (Leviticus 9:3 KJV)

This is the statute of the law, which the Lord hath commanded, saying: Speak unto the children of Israel, that they bring thee a red heifer, faultless, wherein is no blemish, and upon which never came yoke. (Numbers 19:2 Holy Scriptures) "Without spot" means sinless, pure. "Faultless" means no error or wrong act or mistake. The soul/mind is sinless in other words. "Without blemish" means without any physical defects. The innocent lamb would be the innocent symbolic representation of Jesus the Lamb of God who was to come later, the second Adam the savior to restore life and to conquer the destroyer of life. *But now Christ has come, high priest of good things already in being. The tent of his priesthood is a greater and more perfect one, not made by man's hands, that is, not belonging to this created world; the blood of his sacrifice is his own blood, not the blood of goats and calves; and thus he has entered the sanctuary once and for all and secured an eternal deliverance. For if the blood of goats and bulls and the sprinkled ashes of a heifer have power to hollow those who have been defiled and restore their external purity, how much greater is the power of the blood of Christ; he offered himself without blemish to God, a spiritual and eternal sacrifice; and his blood will cleanse our conscience from the deadness of our former ways and fit us for the service of the living God.* (Hebrews 9:11-14 The New English Bible)

God sent His only son, Jesus, to redeem man from his sins once and for all and to reconcile, and some use the same term for the animals, redeem them as well or restore them back to God. To be redeemed as defined in the dictionary means "to buy or pay off, clear by payment: to buy back as after a mortgage, to recover, to convert something for something else, to discharge or fulfill, to make up for, make amends for, to obtain the release or restoration of, as by paying a ransom. To deliver from sin and its consequences by means of a sacrifice offered for the sinner." Thus the restoration of man and animals is through the sacrifice Jesus made for man's salvation and animals restoration back to God. We can not pay for or purchase salvation. Salvation is a gift of grace from our loving Father. It is free and no amount of money can pay to get someone to heaven. Jesus paid that price on the cross and he paid that price for our souls and the restoration of the remainder of creation under the dominion of man.

Redemption can mean delivered from and is not necessarily referring to acts of sin as in the case of animals their fall being the result of man's sin, thus their restoration or redemption is linked to the redemption/restoration of man back to God, through the redeemer, Jesus Christ. *He that overcometh shall inherit all things; and I will be his God, and he shall be my son.* (Revelation 21:7 KJV)

In my opinion whatever we may have to go through now is less than nothing compared with the magnificent future God has in store for us. The whole creation is on tiptoe to see the wonderful sight of the sons of God coming into their own. The world of creation cannot as yet see reality, not because it chooses to be blind, but because in God's purpose it has been so limited—yet it has been given hope. And the hope is that in the end the whole of created life will be rescued from the tyranny of change and decay, and have its share in that magnificent liberty which can only belong to the children of God! It is plain to anyone with eyes to see that at the present time all created life groans in a sort of universal travail. And it is plain, too, that we who have a foretaste of the Spirit are in a state of painful tension, while we wait for the redemption of our bodies which will mean that we have realized our full sonship in him. We were saved by this hope, and let us remember that hope always means waiting for something that we do not yet see. For whoever hopes when he can see? But if we hope for something we cannot see, then we must settle down to wait for it in patience. (Romans 8:18-22 The New Testament in Modern English, Student Edition)

Hope means "assurance"—the promise from God's word that it will happen. Redeemed man and all of the remainder of creation will be restored back to God. All will have a new immortal body.

The following manuscripts from the Dead Sea Scrolls are consistent with Romans 8:23, which speaks of the redemption (renewing) of the physical body, and Revelation 5:13, which speaks of the praise of all creation to God and the Lamb forever and ever.

The Dead Sea Scrolls Uncovered
The Messianic and Visionary Recitals

The manuscript appears to be Ezekiel's vision of the new heaven.

(9) Now behold, a city will be built for the Name of the Great One, {the Eternal Lord}...{And no} (10) evil shall be committed in the pres-

ence of the Great One, {the Eternal Lord...(11) Then the Great One, the
Eternal Lord, will remember His creation {for the purpose of
Good}...{Blessing and honor and praise} (12) {be to} the Great One, the
Eternal Lord.

The New Jerusalem (40554) Plate 3: (4) the time of Righteousness
has come, and the earth will be full of Knowledge and praise of God. (6)
The Ways of God and the mightiness of His works; {they shall be instructed
un}til all Eternity. All cr{eation} (7) will bless Him, and every man will
bow down before him in worship, and their he{arts will be} as one.

Fragment 1 Column 2: (1) {...The Hea}vens and the earth will
obey His Messiah, (2)...and all th}at is in them.

In whom also we have obtained an inheritance, being predestinated
according to the purpose of him who worketh all things after the counsel of
his own will.   (Ephesians 1:11 KJV)

Who is the image of the invisible God, the firstborn of every creature:
For by him were all things created, that are in heaven, and that are in the
earth, visible and invisible, whether they be thrones, or dominions, or
principalities, or powers: all things were created by him, and for him:
And he is before all things, and by him all things consist. And he is the
head of the body, the church: who is the beginning, the firstborn from the
dead; that in all things he might have the preeminence. For it pleased the
Father that in him should all fullness dwell; And, having made peace
through the blood of his cross, by him to reconcile all things unto himself;
by him, I say, whether they be things in earth, or things in heaven.
(Colossians 1:15-20 KJV)

Then I saw a Lamb, looking as if it had been slain, standing in the
center of the throne, encircled by the four living creatures and the elders.
He had seven horns and seven eyes, which are the seven spirits of God sent
out into all the earth. He came and took the scroll from the right hand of
him who sat on the throne. And when he had taken it, the four living
creatures and the twenty-four elders fell down before the Lamb. (Christ).
Each one had a harp and they were holding golden bowls full of incense,
which are the prayers of the saints. And they sang a new song: "You are

worthy to take the scroll and to open its seals, because you were slain, and with your blood you purchased men for God from every tribe and language and people and nation. You have made them to be a kingdom and priests to serve our God, and they will reign on the earth." Then I looked and heard the voice of many angels, numbering thousands upon thousands, and ten thousand times ten thousand. They encircled the throne and the living creatures and the elders. In a loud voice they sang: "Worthy is the Lamb, who was slain, to receive power and wealth and wisdom and strength and honor and glory and praise!" Then I heard every creature in heaven and on earth and under the earth and in the sea, and all that is in them, singing: "To him who sits on the throne and to the Lamb be praise and honor and glory and power, for ever and ever!" The four living creatures said, "Amen," and the elders fell down and worshiped.
(Revelation 5:6-14 Good News Bible)

In Rev. 5:12, Jesus is subordinate to God but closer to Him than all creatures. He alone is worthy to take the earth back from Satan. The angels, saints and all the creatures recognize Jesus as having the power to take the earth back from Satan and are rejoicing together. Matthew Henry's commentary helps explain:

I. The apostle beholds this book taken into the hands of the Lord Jesus Christ. His place and station. He was on the same throne with the Father. Christ, as man and Mediator, is subordinate to God the Father, but is nearer to him than all the creatures. The form in which he appeared. Before he is called a lion; here he appears as a lamb slain. He is a lion to conquer Satan, a lamb to satisfy the justice of God. (as v. 5), he prevailed by his merit and worthiness.

II. No sooner had Christ received this book out of the Father's hand than he received the applause and adoration of angels and men, yea, of every creature. 2. The church begins the doxology, as being more immediately concerned in it (v. 8). (1) The object of their worship—the Lamb, the Lord Jesus Christ, Thou are worthy to take the book, and to open the seals thereof. They mention his suffering; "Thou wast slain." The fruits of his sufferings. {1} Redemption to

God. {2} High exaltation, v. 10. 2. The doxology is carried on by the angels, v. 11. They are said to be innumerable, and to be the attendants of the throne of God. Though they did not need a Savior themselves, yet they rejoice in the redemption and salvation of sinners, and they agree with the church that he is worthy to receive power, and riches, and wisdom, and strength, and honour, and glory, and blessing. 3. This doxology is resounded by the whole creation, v.13. Heaven and earth ring with the high praises of the Redeemer. The whole creation fares the better for Christ. The part which is made for the whole creation is a song of blessing, and honour, and glory, and power. To him that sits on the throne, to God the Father. To the Lamb, the Mediator of the new covenant. We worship and glorify one and the same God for our creation and for our redemption. Thus we have seen this sealed book passing with great solemnity from the hand of the Creator into the hand of the Redeemer. (Rev.5:6-14, Matthew Henry's Commentary)

Let everything he has made give praise to him. For he issued his command, and they came into being; he established them forever and forever. His orders will never be revoked. (Psalm 148:5-6 TLB)

And all flesh shall see the salvation of God. (Luke 3:6 KJV)

Isaiah 11:6-9 refers to both those of the human race who are now enemies and also of the animal kingdom who are at present natural enemies as being at peace with each other in heaven:

The wolf also shall dwell with the lamb, and the leopard shall lie down with the kid; and the calf and the young lion and the fatling together; and a little child shall lead them. And the cow and the bear shall feed; their young ones shall lie down together: and the lion shall eat straw like the ox. And the suckling child shall play on the hole of the asp, and the weaned child shall put his hand on the cockatrice's den. They shall not hurt nor destroy in all my holy mountain: for the earth shall be full of the knowledge of the Lord, as the waters cover the sea. (Isaiah 11:6-9 KJV)

In heaven all flesh—all creation—will bless His (God's) holy name as they will also the Messiah (Jesus).

The Dead Sea Scrolls Uncovered
The Splendor of the Spirits

Manuscript B Fragment 1: *(9) and all the servants of Ho{liness...} (10) in the Perfection of th{eir] works...(11) in {their} wond{rous} Temples...(12) {a}ll {their} servant[s...} (13) Your Holiness in the habitat{ion of...}* Fragment 2 (1)*...them, and they shall bless Your Holy Name with blessing{s}... (2) and they shall bless} you, all creatures of flesh in unison, whom {You} have creat{ed}...(3) be}asts and birds and reptiles and the fish of the seas, and all...(4) {Y}ou have created them all anew...*Fragment 3 (13)*...The Holy Spirit {sett}led upon His Messiah...*

Do not dread death's sentence; remember those who came before you and those who will come after. This is the sentence passed on all living creatures by the Lord, so why object to what seems good to the Most High? Whether your life lasts ten or a hundred or a thousand years, its length will not be held against you in Sheol, Hell. (Ecclesiasticus 41:3-4 NJV)

The Book of Wisdom is believed to in part be written by Solomon and refers to him speaking on wisdom and life. *For your great power is always at your service, and who can withstand the might of your arm? The whole world, for you, can no more than tip a balance, like a drop of morning dew falling on the ground. Yet you are merciful to all, because you are almighty, you overlook people's sins, so that they can repent. Yes, you love everything that exists, and nothing that you have made disgusts you, since, if you had hated something, you would not have made it. And how could a thing subsist, had you not willed it? Or how be preserved, if not called forth by you? No, you spare all, since all is yours, Lord, lover of life?* (Wisdom 11:21-26 NJV) *For your imperishable spirit is in everything.* (12:1 Wisdom NJV)

Whom do we fear? Luke says: *I tell you, my friends, do not be afraid of those who kill the body but cannot afterward do anything worse.*

I will show you whom to fear: fear God, who, after killing, has the authority to throw into hell. Believe me, he is the one you must fear! Aren't five sparrows sold for two pennies? Yet not one sparrow is forgotten by God. (Luke 12:4-16 Good News Bible)

This message of God from the lips of Jesus stated that after one is dead, God has the power to send him to hell. It does not say God kills. It was Satan who came to kill, steal and destroy as God never wanted any of His creation to be lost, to fall and to suffer. But after the killing of the body brought on by man in his disobedience to God, in which God said if man sins he will surely die, God has the power to throw him into hell. So fear or reverence the Lord. God said those who are his children He will remember. They will be with Him in heaven forever. Those who are not adopted into His kingdom, through their own choice to choose Satan as their father over God, He will forget. What does the scripture say about the sparrows? Not one of them, even though lowly creation below man, so lowly that you can purchase them for two pennies, yet they will not be forgotten by God. He will remember His creation for good as scripture says. They, even the sparrows will be in heaven as God will not forget them.

For God did not make death, he takes no pleasure in destroying the living. To exist; for this he created all things: the creatures of the world have health in them. In them is no fatal poison, and Hades has no power over the world: for uprightness is immortal but the godless call for Death with deed and word counting him friend, they wear themselves out for him, with him they make a pact, worthy as they are to belong to him. (Wisdom 1:13-16 NJV)

Only the sinful, unrepentant of mankind need fear death; God through Jesus will restore all the creatures and repentant man.

God is part of Creation. Creation is part of Him, part of His eternal existence. He breathes life into all creation and that life is sustained. The spirit and soul receive a renewed, immortal body of youth, health, and perfection, one of everlasting beauty. All creation will be renewed in the same way. We will all be wiser, more glorious, more in love with each other and God. Creation will be perfect in every way never dying. The hope is for all creation as Romans says. It will be a return to perfection as in the Garden of Eden. I have read of many who have been in some way caught up in heaven and they say it is a glorified version of earth. What is true in heaven is also true of earth.

The first heaven and the first earth will pass away, as the scripture says, but that does not mean that they disappear. There will be a new heaven and a new earth, the renewal of heaven and earth. It is not a replacement of them. We remain soul and spirit as do all creatures but we will have renewed bodies, which will be as our old ones only without spot or blemish. God does not create a new person. He keeps the old one but He restores the old one to a perfect pre-sin state. We will be perfect, all creation, all creatures will be perfect and we will physically recognize each other as we do on earth. We have never known what is has been like to be perfect to look perfect to love perfectly, to enjoy life with absolutely nothing to worry about, to live without pain. That is what the new creature and the new creation will be like. God is restoring His creation.

Then I saw a new heaven and a new earth; for the first heaven and the first earth had passed away... (Revelation 21:1 KJV)

Richard Bauckham, author of *The Theology of the Book of Revelations,* states: "The contrast between 'the first heaven and the first earth', on the one hand, and 'the new heaven and the new earth', on the other, refers to the eschatological (means or system of) renewal of this creation, not its replacement by another. He compares the flood as a reversion of creation to the chaos from which it was first created. Revelation 21:5 says *'Behold, I make all things new.'"*

Included in *Animal Theology* by Dr. Andrew Linzey is a profound statement by Paulos Mar Gregorios. Dr. Gregorios was Principal of Orthodox Theological Seminary in Kottyam, Kerala, Metropolitan of Delhi in the Indian Orthodox Church, author of numerous books and former president of the World Council of Churches. He stated: "Christ, the Beloved Son, is the manifest presence (icon) of the unmanifest God. He is the Elder Brother of all things created, for it was by him and in him that all things were created, whether here on earth in the sensible world or in the world beyond the horizon of your senses which we call heaven.

"That includes you, who were once alienated, enemies in your own minds/souls to God's purpose, immersed in evil actions; but now you are bodily reconciled in his fleshly body which has tasted death. Christ intends to present you holy, spotless, and blameless in God's presence, if you remain firm in the faith, rooted and grounded in him, unswerving from the hope of the good news you have heard. The good news that is declared not only to men and women on earth, but also to all created beings under heaven. It is this gospel that Paul has also been called to serve. (1) Christ himself should be seen in his three principal relationships: (1) to members incorporated in his body, (2) to the human race, and (3) to the other than human order of created existence in a many-planed universe. Each of these is related to the other."

Flavius Josephus and His Discourse to the Greeks on Heaven and Hell

Flavius Josephus was born Joseph Ben Metthias. He came from an aristocratic priestly family in Jerusalem. He was of high regard in intellectual circles and by the age of fourteen, high priests consulted him in matters of Jewish law. He was born ca. 37 A.D. and died ca. 100 A.D. in Rome. His discourse to the Greeks concerning Hades includes not only the fate of man but of angels and animals as well. Coming from an aristocratic priestly Jewish family, he understood the scriptures of the Old Testament and the meaning of Christ and his sacrifice for mankind. Josephus spoke of the restrictions of eating the flesh of animals which still had the life-blood in them, explaining it contained their spirit and soul. He also spoke of death, the risen spirit and soul and the future resurrection of the body, which though it had gone into the ground still remained part of the earth, not perishing but one day to be restored to a new perfection reunited with the soul and spirit which had ascended to heaven if it be a righteous person; and if unrighteous, the old, sick body unchanged would be reunited with the soul and spirit doomed to eternal torment. As a great scholar of the scriptures and one who walked close to God he understood the resurrection of the animals as well as righteous people, explaining through his writing in this his commentary.

In point 6 of Josephus's "Discourse To The Greeks Concerning Hades" he says, "For all men, the just as well as the unjust, shall be brought before God the word: for to him hath the Father committed all judgment: and he, in order to fulfill the will of his Father, shall come as Judge, whom we call Christ. For Minos and Rhadamanthus are not the judges, as you Greeks do suppose, but he whom God the Father hath glorified: Concerning Whom We Have Elsewhere Given A More Particular Account, For The Sake Of Those Who Seek After Truth. This person, exercising the righteous judgment of the Father towards all men, hath prepared a just sentence for every one, according to his works; at whose judgment-seat when all men, and angels, and demons shall stand, they will send forth one voice, and say, JUST IS THY JUDGMENT; the rejoinder to which will bring a just sentence upon both parties, by giving justly to those that (who) have done well an everlasting fruition but allotting to the lovers of wicked works eternal punishment. To these belong the unquenchable fire, and that without end, and a certain fiery worm, never dying, and not destroying the body, but continuing its eruption out of the body with never-ceasing grief: neither will sleep give ease to these men, nor will the night afford them comfort; death will not free them from their punishment, nor will the interceding prayers of their kindred profit them; for the just are no longer seen by them, nor are they thought worthy of remembrance. But the just shall remember only their righteous actions, whereby they have attained the heavenly kingdom, in which there is no sleep, no sorrow, no corruption, no care, no night, no day measured by time, no sun driven in his course along the circle of heaven by necessity, and measuring out the bounds and conversions of the seasons, for the better illumination of the life of men; no moon decreasing and increasing, or introducing a variety of seasons, nor will she then moisten the earth, no burning sun, no Bear turning round [the pole], no Orion to rise, no wandering of innumerable stars. The earth will not then be difficult to be passed over, nor will it be hard to find out the court of paradise, nor will there be any fearful roaring of the sea, forbidding the passengers to walk on it; even that will be made easily passable to the just, though it will not be void of moisture. Heaven will not then be uninhabitable by men, and it will not be impossible to discover the way of ascending thither (other side/far side). The earth will not be uncultivated, nor require too much labor of men, but will bring forth its fruits of its own accord, and will be well adorned with them. There will be no more generations of wild beasts, nor will the substance of the rest of the animals shoot out any more; for it will not produce men, (in other words there will be no new birth of animals or men but which have been born from the beginning of creation will continue on) but the number of the righteous will continue, and never fail, together with righteous angels, and spirits [of God], and with his word, as a choir of righteous men and women that never grow old, and continue in an incorruptible state, singing hymns to God, who hath advanced them to that happiness, by the means of a regular institution of life; with whom the whole creation also will lift up a perpetual hymn from corruption, to incorruption, as glorified by a splendid and pure spirit. It will not then be restrained by a bond of necessity, but with a lively freedom shall offer up a voluntary hymn, and shall praise him that made them, together with the angels, and spirits, and men now freed from bondage.

[The Bible reminds us that animals, all creation belongs to God and though we are caretakers of the animals, we are not their owners.

*For every beast of the forest is mine, and the cattle upon a thousand hills.
I know all the fowls of the mountains: and the wild beasts of the field are
mine.* (Psalm 50:9-10) — MBP]

From the Virginia Christian Israelites comes a prayer by Robert
A. Everett:

"We praise you for the creation of the world and all the living
creatures in the earth, sky and sea. We are thankful, O God. For the
bond between all living creatures created by the same author, and
for memory of our kinship to the animal world kindled each time a
rainbow appears. We are thankful, O God. Keep us mindful of the
vision of the peaceable kingdom in which all living creatures dwell
in harmony. This we pray, O God. Give us eyes to see our responsi-
bilities, not just to the human community, but to the community of
all living creatures. Help us to see, O God. In this world of violence
and unkindness, let us act in a gentle way towards all your creatures.
A simple stroke on a dog's head, a scratch on a cat's chin. Help us to
be gentle, O God. Help us to lessen the suffering of your creatures,
O God. Hasten the coming of your kingdom when the sun will
shine on all your creation living in peace and love. We pray this, O
Lord. Help us to be kind and gentle like our Lord Jesus..."

To summarize all that is said within *Animals, Immortal Beings*, it
is evidenced by the most recognizable founders of all Christian faiths
from Protestantism to Roman Catholicism that animals are immortal beings which possess a soul or spirit, are sinless, with many functioning as helpmates to man. They are to be treated as God's creatures, not ours, and as stewards of God's creation we are to govern,
provide, and treat them humanely in whatever capacity each animal
serves. The Bible does say they have been and still are used in sacrificial ways for man, even to their death, yet they are never to be
tortured, and never needlessly injured or killed. And man must recognize that we will one day be accountable to God for any pain and

abuse we have inflicted upon His non-human animals should we not repent of this sin.

Who could think that a real, all-loving God would annihilate all of the lower animals that have suffered for man and his sins? How devastating in the eyes of God it is to see loving and knowledgeable people hear that God and His son are evil destroyers of sentient, loving beings who have never had a chance for happiness in this world and preach that they never will. Many people end up rejecting all offers to come to salvation due to our ignorant biblically uneducated, and callous ways. We, as Christian writers and ministers in understanding biblical truths concerning the immortality of animals, want all to know of God's love for both man and beast.

(1) And there was a man of the Pharisees, named Nicodemus, a ruler for the Jews. (2) This man came to Jesus by night, and said to him: Rabbi, we know that thou art come a teacher from God; for no man can do these signs which thou dost, unless God be with him. (3) Jesus answered, and said to him: Amen, amen I say to thee, unless a man be born again, he cannot see the kingdom of God. (4) Nicodemus saith to him: How can a man be born when he is old? Can he enter a second time into his mother's womb, and be born again? (5) Jesus answered: Amen, amen I say to thee, unless a man be born again of water and the Holy Ghost, he cannot enter into the kingdom of God. (6) That which is born of the flesh, is flesh; and that which is born of the Spirit, is spirit. (7) Wonder not, that I said to thee, you must be born again. (16) For God so loved the world, as to give his only begotten Son; that whosoever believeth in him, may not perish, but may have life everlasting. (17) for God sent not his Son into the world, to judge the world, but that the world may be saved by him. (John 3:1-7, 15-16 Douay Rheims Bible)

Heaven's Countryside
by Robert S. Clark

Somehow I can't help but feel that
All those pets I ever loved and lost
Someway made the journey across
To the other side.
And even now they're playing
With the children in heaven's countryside.
It's there from Genesis to Revelation
Our Father's love knows no boundaries
For you, or me, or these
Who are also His creation.
Above all else the Lord's heart is tender
So how is it we can render
Those who He brought through the flood
And gathered 'round His manger
Of no eternal consequence
When their life in this world is finished
And who are we, if not dreamers
If we think it's left to us to decide
Who may or may not enter heaven's countryside.

(Used by permission)

God and his son Jesus love all creation. All the animals will be in heaven but man has a choice. Please make sure you make the choice and choose Jesus. He did give his life for you. We are all sinners but there is no sin that cannot be forgiven. Just turn to Jesus so you can join your beloved pets in heaven.

Bibliography

Bibles and Commentaries Referenced

Criswell, W. A., editor. *Criswell Study Bible*, Authorized King James Version. Nashville: Thomas Nelson, 1979.

Darby, John Nelson, translator. *Darby Bible*. Old Testament, 1890. New Testament, 1884. Translated by R. A. Huebner. Pleasant Truth Publishers, 1994

Eisenman, Robert and Michael Wise, translators. *The Dead Sea Scrolls Uncovered*. New York: Barnes & Noble, 1992.

Douay Rheims Bible, first published by the English College at Douay; Old Testament 1609, New Testament First 1582. Rockford, IL: Tan Books and Publishers, Inc., 1899. (no reprinting date given).

King James Version of the Holy Bible. The World Publishing Co. Cleveland, New York. 1945.

American Bible Society, *Good News Bible*, New York 1976.

Holy Scriptures According to the Masoretic Text. Philadelphia: Jewish Publications Society of America, 1958.

Living Bible. Wheaton, IL: Tyndale House Publishers, 1971.

New American Bible Saint Joseph Edition. New York: Catholic Book Publishing Company, 1970.

New English Bible with the Apocrypha, Second Edition. Oxford University Press and Cambridge University Press, 1961,1970.

New Jerusalem Bible. New York: Doubleday, 1990.

The Student Bible, New International Version. Grand Rapids, MI: Zonderrvan, 1986.

Phillips, J. B., translator. *New Testament in Modern English, Student Edition*. New York: Macmillan Publishing Company, 1996.

Bibliography

Henry, Matthew (1662-1714). *Commentary* (NIV Version). Grand Rapids, MI: Zondervan, 1992.

Open Bible. Wheaton, IL: Tyndale House Publishers, 1974.

Revised Standard Version. New York: American Bible Society, 1971.

Revised Standard Version — Old Testament. Camden, NJ: Thomas Nelson & Sons, 1964.

Saint Joseph New Catholic Edition Holy Bible. New York: Catholic Book Publishing Company, 1961.

Strong, James, LL.D., S.T.D. *Strong's Exhaustive Concordance of the Bible.* Nashville, Camden, Kansas City: Thomas Nelson, 1990.

The Jewish Bible TANAKH The Holy Scriptures: The new JPS Translat ion according to the Traditional Hebrew Text; Torah / Nevim / Kethuvim. The Jewish Publication Society Philadelphia, 1999.

Books Referenced

Al-Hafiz, B.A. Masri. "Animal Experimentation: The Muslim Viewpoint" Quotations from the Quran, Hadith, and customary law, the Quran dating back to 610-632, the Hadith dating 632-656. Published in *Animals Sacrifices*, edited by Tom Regan. Philadelphia: Temple University Press, 1986.

Battles, Ford Lewis and Andre Malan Huyg. *Calvin's Commentary on Seneca de Clementia.* Leiden, The Netherlands: E. J. Brill, 1969.

Bauckham, Richard. *The Theology of the Book of Revelation.* New York and Cambridge in the U.K.: Cambridge University Press, 1993.

Beecham, John. *Sermons on Several Occasions, Vol. II.* London: Wesleyan Conference Office, 1874.

Bouwsma, William J. *John Calvin.* New York, Oxford University Press, 1989.

Buddemeyer-Porter, Mary. *Will I See Fido in Heaven?* St. Louis, MO: Eden Publications, 1995, 2001, 2004.

Carroll, James, The Very Reverend. Commentary on *Merciful God, Merciless Man* from a sermon. Used by permission.

Clark, Robert S. *Heaven's Countryside.* Homestead, FL, copyright 1992. Used by permission.

Curnock, Nehemiah, editor, *The Journal of the Rev. John Wesley, A.M., Volume III: A Bicentenary Issue.* London: The Epworth Press, 1938.

Curnock, Nehemiah, editor. *The Journal of the Rev. John Wesley, A.M., Volume IV: A Bicentenary Issue.* London: The Epworth Press, 1938

Everett, Robert. *Virginia Christian Israelites.* Round Hill, Virginia, 2001.

Free, Ann Cottrell, editor. *Animals, Nature and Albert Schweitzer.* Washington, DC: Flying Fox Publications, 1988.

Goudge, Elizabeth. *My God and My All: The Life of Francis of Assisi.* New York: Coward-McCann, Inc., 1959.

Harker, Jeff. *The Spirit of the Animal.* Research report, 2001.

Hartley, David. *Observations on Man: His Frame, His Duty, and His Expectations. 2 vols.* Bath and London: Samual Richardson 1749.

Harwood, Dix. *Love for Animals.* Doctoral dissertation, Columbia University, New York, 1928. Includes *Luther: Lectures on Romans* from pages 235 through 259 of his *Lectures of Romans* text original translations and *Luther's Works: Lectures on Romans, European Magazine,* 1784: vi, 354ff.

Hildrop, Rev. John, MA. "Free Thoughts Upon the Brute Creation." *The Ark,* A Publication of The Catholic Study Circle for Animal Welfare. Number 195, Winter 2003.

Hume, David. Edited by L.A. Selby-Bigge. Third ed. Revised by Peter H. Nidditch. *Treatise of Human Nature.* Original publication (anonymous) from 1739-1740, Oxford, Clarendon Press [1748] 1975.

John Paul II. *Crossing the Threshold of Hope.* New York: Random House, Inc., 1994.

John Paul II. *God, Father and Creator: A Catechesis on The Creed, Volume One.* Boston: Pauline Books and Media, 1996.

John Paul II. *Pope John Paul II: In My Own Words*. Compiled and edited by Anthony F. Chiffolo. New York: Gramercy Books, 1998.

John Paul II. *Quotable John Paul II*. Compiled and edited by Mike Towle. Nashville: TowleHouse Publishing, 2003.

Just, Gustave, editor. *The Life of Luther*. St. Louis, MO: Concordia Publishing House, 1903.

Lewis, C.S., editor. *George MacDonald Selections: An Anthology of 365 Readings*. New York: Touchstone, 1996.

Linzey, Andrew. *Animal Theology*. Urbana, IL: University of Illinois Press, 1994.

MacDonald, George. *The Hope of the Gospel*. New York: D. Appleton and Company, 1892.

Morris, Leon. *The Cross of Jesus*. Grand Rapids, MI: Wm. B. Eerdmans Publishing Co., 1988.

Oswald, Hilton C., editor. *Lectures on Romans*. Concordia Publishing House, St. Louis 1972

Parker, Percy Livingstone, editor. "The Journal of John Wesley," *The Tyndale Series of Great Biographies*. Includes an introduction by Hugh Price Hughes and "Appreciation of the Journal of John Wesley" by Augustine Birrell, K.C. Chicago: Moody Press, 1951.

Pauck, Wilhelm, translator and editor. *Martin Luther Lectures on Romans*. New York: West Minister Press, 1961.

Pickthall, Muhammad. *The Glorious Quran*. Des Plaines, IL: Library of Islam, 1994.

Primatt, Dr. Humphry. *The Duty of Mercy and the Sin of Cruelty to B rute Animals*. [1776] Ed. Richard Ryder. Centaur Press, Fontwell, 1992.

The Readers Digest Association, Inc. *Marvels & Mysteries of Our Animal World*. New York: Reader's Digest, 1964.

Schultz, Robert C., editor. *Luther's Works Volume 46: The Christian in Society*. Philadelphia: Fortress Press, 1967.

Schweitzer, Albert. *Philosophy of Civilization.* New York: Macmillan, 1949.

Torrance, D. W., and T. F. Torrance, ET by Ross Mackenzie. *Calvin's Commentaries: The Epistles of Paul the Apostle to the Romans and to the Thessalonians.* London and Edinburgh: Oliver and Boyd, 1961.

Walker, Williston. *Great Men of the Christian Church: John Calvin.* University of Chicago Press, Chicago, 1908.

Other References

A Defense of Calvinism by C.H. Spurgeon:
  http://www.spurgeon.org/calvinis.htm

Burr, David, Professor Emeritus, translator. *Concerning Saint Francis of Assisi and the Animals.*
  http://www.majbill.vt.edu/history/burr/default.html

John Calvin, Theologian by Benjamin B. Warfield:
  http://www.the-highway.com/caltheo_Warfield.html

Josephus, Flavius. An Extract out of *Josephus' Discourse to the Greeks Concerning Hades*:
  http://wesley.nnuedu/josephus/autobiog.htm

The History Learning Site:
  www.historylearningsite.co.uk/calvin.htm

John Wesley, An On-line Exhibition: The John Rylands University Library of Manchester:
  http://rylibweb.man.ac.uk/data1/dg/methodist/jwol1.html

The National Shrine of Saint Francis of Assisi:
  http://www.shrinesf.org/francis_menu.htm

Talmage, Rev. Dr. T. Dewitt. From the collection of his works from 1863-1890, New Jersey, Philadelphia and Brooklyn, N.Y.
  http://www.wheaton.edu/bgc/archives/GUIDES/129.htm

Bibliography

Recommended for Further Study

Animals Have Souls and...Do Go to Heaven (booklet of scriptural references) by Bill LaSalle. Eden Publications, LLC, Manchester, MO.

Animals, Nature and Albert Schweitzer. Edited and with commentary by Ann Cottrell Free, Eden Publications, LLC, Manchester, MO.

Animals On the Agenda and *Animal Theology* by Dr. Andrew Linzey. University of Illinois Press.

Animal Theology by Dr. Andrew Linzey, University of Illinois Press.

I'll See You Again My Friend by Skip Daniels, Eden Publications, LLC, Manchester, MO.

The Immortality of Animals by Dr. Elijah Buckner, Eden Publications, LLC, Manchester, MO.

The Theology of the Book of Revelation by Dr. Richard Bauckham, Cambridge University Press.

When Your Pet Dies by Diane Pomerance, Ph.D., Polaire Publications, Flower Mound, TX.

Will I See Fido in Heaven? by Mary Buddemeyer-Porter. Also available on CD and Audio Cassette as *Will I See My Pet in Heaven?* Eden Publications, LLC, Manchester, MO.

Video: "I'll See You in Heaven My Friend," Eden Publications, LLC, Manchester, MO.

Eden Publications, LLC
P.O. Box 789
Manchester, MO 63011
www.creatures.com

About the Author

MARY BUDDEMEYER-PORTER, author of *Will I See Fido in Heaven?* (audio version, *Will I See My Pet in Heaven?*) is an educator and Christian lecturer appearing on national television, radio and in churches since 1995 concerning the immortality of animals based on the Bible. She has a master's degree in Arts in Education, and received her

theological training at Missouri Baptist College and Maryville University in St. Louis, Missouri and for over fifteen years her focus of study and research has been on the immortality of animals based on the Bible. She is also the co-founder of Eden Publications, a Christian publishing company that publishes and distributes Christian-based books on the immortality of animals.

She donates much time in grief counseling for pet owners and is a consultant for new authors who have written books from a Christian perspective on the immortality of animals.

Mary is a member of ASCAP and has been the producer for two children's television series and is a Regional Emmy-nominated songwriter. She is the president of Note Family, Inc. and gives seminars on the *Land of Music* music education system she co-created. She has taught in private Christian schools, public schools and college.

Mary is married with two grown sons and two step-children whose families all are involved with helping the homeless animals of the world. Her family also includes four rescue dogs. She was born on a farm in northern Missouri where she learned to care for and love all the creatures that came into her life.

Author Portrait by Roman Buddemeyer